invincible irishman

A Biography of Percy T. Magan

Formerly "For God and C.M.E."
Abridged

by Merlin L. Neff

PACIFIC PRESS PUBLISHING ASSOCIATION
Mountain View, California

Omaha, Nebraska

Introduction

Occasionally a man and an institution interact to the extent that ever afterward they are associated in the minds of those who knew them both. This was the case with Percy T. Magan and the College of Medical Evangelists. Dr. Magan was a man of wit, of energy, and of perseverance. He had a vision of what the College of Medical Evangelists should become. To help it grow and develop he willingly devoted his time, his forceful personality, and his many other talents.

This book presents the story of this gifted man, giving a vivid picture of his life and work. So far as words can go in recreating the living spirit of an individual, this book does so. Those who knew Percy T. Magan will again come under the spell of the personality which made him outstanding. Those who never met him will still find him well worth knowing vicariously, by means of Dr. Merlin Neff's gifted pen.

Dr. Neff and Dr. Magan were close personal friends. In addition, Dr. Neff thoroughly acquainted himself with Dr. Magan's writings, speeches, and letters. He has captured for us the personal charm, the Irish sense of humor, and the intense drive of the man who cajoled, good-naturedly browbeat, and otherwise persuaded those who were able to contribute something—money, time, or talent—to the program of the school. He has made Dr. Magan stand out, not as a mere historical figure in our denominational annals, but as a man of flesh and blood.

This biography, recording some of the early history of the College of Medical Evangelists and of the man who gave himself so enthusiastically and vigorously for its growth and development, will fill a long-felt need.

G. T. Anderson

Library of Congress Catalog Card No. 64-16798

Litho in U.S.A.

Contents

1

A Lad From the Irish Gentry

The chill November wind struck Marlfield House in temperamental gusts, pelting the windows with heavy raindrops; but the brick, stone, and well-seasoned wood in the walls stood bravely against the storm. The spacious three-storied mansion, with its thirteen bedrooms, staffed with a dozen house servants, was surrounded by woods and open fields bordered with yew hedges. The estate was less than four miles from the village of Gorey in County Wexford, which lies at the southeastern tip of Ireland.

Lights burned brightly in Marlfield House at this early morning hour, as nurse Ferguson opened the bedroom door to listen to the gasps of her mistress in the pains of labor. Catherine Ann Richards-Magan could be seen in the dim yellow light of the lamp when the nurse raised it above her head to catch a glimpse of the taut face of the expectant mother.

"May the saints rest you, ma'am," comforted the servant. "The doctor should be coming any moment now, providing the storm doesn't slow his horse."

A faint smile of recognition could be seen on Mistress Magan's face. This was not her first ordeal in childbirth, for there was little Emily, the elder child, who at this moment lay sleeping in the nursery on the floor below. The expected baby must be a boy, the woman decided in the minutes between her pains, for a son would please his father.

"Where is the master?" Catherine asked with a sigh.

"He's in the study, walking and fretting as all men do in such times," answered nurse Ferguson, a bit of acid in her voice.

Hearing footsteps in the hall, the servant turned to find the doctor with Rosie, the kitchen maid, close behind, carrying a kettle of hot water.

"It's a boy, master," announced nurse Ferguson, entering the library with a blanketed bundle in her arms.

"Then a happy day it is!" Percy Magan exclaimed. "He shall be called Percy Tilson Magan." With clumsy fingers the father pushed aside the edge of the blanket to look at the tiny face. "Quite a lad ye are, Percy. Now don't pucker and cry; you've too much Irish spunk for that."

A BOY IN THE FAMILY

Percy Tilson Magan, born November 13, 1867, came from a family of the Irish gentry. His grandfather, George Magan, had married Ellen O'Connor, a descendant of Ruaidri Va Conchubair, called Roderic (Rory) O'Connor, the king of Connaught and from 1166 high king of Ireland, who in the summer of 1170 rose to the defense of the Irish against a Norman invasion. When Henry II of England invaded Ireland with an imposing army in 1171, many tribal kings paid homage to him, but not the kings of Connaught and Ulster. It was four years before the Treaty of Windsor was signed, making O'Connor king of Connaught under the king of England.

Civil strife, war with England, and religious conflict flared again and again through the centuries, a constant unrest which gave Ireland the epithet "the trembling sod." The strong animosity between Roman Catholicism and Protestantism, which seemed to thrive on Irish soil, was felt in the Magan family. When Percy's grandfather, George Magan, was wed to Ellen O'Connor, the marriage agreement stated that all sons born to the union should be raised as Protestants, while all daughters were to be Catholics. The story comes down in the family that when Percy (the father of Percy T.) was born, his zealous sister, Monica, surreptitiously bundled him up and rushed to the priest to have him christened a Roman Catholic; but when the Protestant father heard of his daughter's action, he thrashed her soundly and then took his newborn son to the Protestant bishop to be "deconsecrated." Thus the father of Percy T. began his days in conflict, and his life was ever tumultuous.

Deeply prejudiced against Catholicism, Percy became an introvert with few social interests. He fell in love with Catherine Ann Richards, whose ancestors were Huguenots. Her father was an Anglican bishop and her uncle, Solemn Richards, was president of the Royal Society of Surgeons of Ireland.

By the time Percy Tilson was born, his father owned only a small portion of the vast original estates that the Magans once possessed. Indeed, the senior Magan rented Marlfield House, whose stately shade trees and broad lawns, inviting paths and dusky woods, patios and rustic seats, made an ideal playground for the growing children.

There was a pond where young Percy, accompanied by Rosie, sailed his toy boat. In addition to the elder sister, there were younger girls, for Rachel, Muriel, and Violet were born during Percy's childhood. And when he was fourteen, another brother, Arthur T. Shaen, was added to the family.

On rainy days the young children played in the third-floor nursery, and Percy remembered the broad open stairway with its inviting banisters. There was a long scratch on the wood and a scar on the boy's anatomy after one particular slide when a button on his pants got in the way! On sunny days Percy sometimes walked to Courtown harbor, about five miles from Gorey, to watch the fishermen with their nets. Indeed, the lure of the sea infiltrated Marlfield House, for a piece of wreckage of a fishing boat the master once owned was set in an honored place on the front lawn. The vessel had been the victim of a storm, and old Paddy Doran, the keeper, who lived in a lodge near the gate of the estate, had been aboard the craft when it was wrecked.

The usual pranks of youth were attached to Percy's name. One day as he was looking out the nursery window, he knocked a potted geranium from the ledge, and it crashed on the walk, narrowly missing his sister. Again he almost caused a tragedy in the family when he let go of the baby carriage in which his sister Muriel was sleeping, and it rolled down the path toward the lily pond, stopping on the brink of the pool as if checked by a guardian angel.

Percy's father and mother sometimes gave elaborate dinners, and the boy and his sister would be allowed to come downstairs for dessert. With the soup, fish, game, and roast beef courses completed, and only the pudding course left, the hungry boy did not feel he shared much of the banquet. One night, when the feast was over, Percy and his sister were sent with the ladies into the drawing room, while the men sat in the large dining room. Finally, when the gentlemen joined the ladies in the drawing room, the lad and his sister were told to kiss everyone good-night and go to bed. The seven-year-old boy and six-year-old girl made their way to the huge sideboard in the dining room, on which were wines, champagne, and hard liquor. Percy pushed a dining-room chair over to the sideboard, climbed up on it, and solemnly asked his sister what she would like to drink. When she chose champagne, he filled two large goblets with the bubbly liquid and gave one to her and with the other clasped in both hands proceeded to fill himself with the beverage. Whalen, the butler, appeared at the dining room door, and in stentorian tones said, "Master Percy, I will tell your father on you."

The quick-witted boy answered back, "That's all right, Whalen, and I'll tell him I saw you under the lime tree the other night kissing and hugging Jane Belle, the cook. Then you'll get fired." Discipline was strict in those days, and lovemaking among servants was absolutely taboo. A quick compromise was reached, and the butler carried the boy and his sister, slightly intoxicated, up three flights of stairs to the nursery, where nurse Ferguson and Rosie tucked the adventurers into bed.

Discipline was necessary to restrain the lively Irish lad. In a fit of temper at his governess, whom he detested, Percy jumped on the woman's trailing skirt and loosened the waistband, which caused no end of embarrassment! His father, returning from a ride, happened on the scene and punished his son with a riding whip.

SCHOOL DAYS IN ENGLAND

It was the custom for the Irish gentry to have a private tutor for their sons before they sent them to select schools in England. At the age of ten, Percy was informed that he was to go to a military school for a more formal education. It was not easy for the boy to break with his home, for he dearly loved his mother and nurse Ferguson, the widow of a British admiral, who gave young Magan a medal of honor that her husband had received for bravery in the Royal Navy.

The austere father took his son to Dublin, where they embarked on a ship sailing across the Irish Sea to England. It was Percy's first ocean voyage, and his eyes and ears absorbed the new and wondrous scenes and sounds of thriving cities, busy docks, ships in port, and the rolling sea. To the city of Chester traveled father and son to enroll Percy at Arnold House, a proprietary school for boys nine to twelve years of age. In addition to the headmaster, there were usually four other men on the teaching staff as well as "visiting masters." The lad was homesick and without friends or relatives. Indeed, his loneliness was so acute that for a time he went to his room each day for a "crying spell."

Chester, one of the oldest of English cities, was founded as the Roman station of Deva, about A.D. 48, on the river Dee, some sixteen miles south of Liverpool. This station became a bulwark against hostile tribes from North Wales, and a center of trade with Ireland. Still standing today around the old city is the Roman wall, twenty feet thick and two miles in length. The Tudor architecture of the ancient buildings interested Percy, and he enjoyed walking on the balconies that extended from the second stories over the narrow streets. These unusual balconies were called "the Rows." The very atmosphere of the town breathed history, and here young Magan absorbed knowledge and reveled in the wonders of the past. From such stimulation, no doubt, grew much of his love for things historical.

As a student at Arnold House School, Percy stood second in his class. However, his petulant father was not pleased with his son's scholarship, for he maintained that if the lad were not lazy he could be first in his studies.

Young Magan's next school was St. George's near Huntingdon, about sixty miles north of London. This institution was presided over by "Old Wix," a typical hot-tempered disciplinarian of the time, who fed the hungry lads "maggoty" ham and stale bread doused in paraffin oil. Percy vividly remembered seeing his cousin flogged until he fainted because the poor lad could not correctly translate a Latin assignment. Later the unconscious boy was carried to the pump and doused with cold water to revive him. Percy barely escaped a flogging himself when he went on a bicycle trip to Huntingdon on an errand for a faculty member. The boy refused to give the names of several fellow students he had seen in town who were off the campus without permission. Young Magan was given the choice of divulging the names of the boys, taking a flogging, or translating Latin for a seemingly interminable number of hours. He chose the Latin!

Memories of the schoolmaster lingered in Magan's mind. Years later he wrote: "Poor Old Wix! I can see his violet nose yet (mauve, I believe you used to call it) as with a look that Satan could not imitate, he would say, 'Come here, little boy, come here; bend over, little boy, bend over,' and then that extended cane of his would whack down on my *gluteus maximus* muscle and raise great blood blisters upon that part of my anatomy which the Lord never intended to be treated that way." When he visited Old Wix in later years, Percy found the headmaster had married a kindhearted woman whose patient nature had influenced her husband to treat the lads with more consideration.

When Percy came home from school, he frequently stopped in Dublin at Marrion Square to visit his aunt and uncle, named Vereker, the parents of Field Marshal Viscount John S. Gort, who distinguished himself in the British army at Malta and Dunkirk during

World War II. On one visit Percy was accompanied by a schoolmate, Charlie Waters (nicknamed Fatty), upon whom he played a joke. Years later the Irishman wrote: "I remember that I had kidded Fatty a lot about seasickness. I don't think he had ever been on the sea before, and I told him if he put a piece of brown paper over his stomach, he would not get seasick. So he got a huge chunk of brown paper and wound it all over his belly. In spite of all that, I think he was sick as a dog. But in the morning when we were walking over to see the Verekers, I was a great swell, and for that matter so was Fatty. We had on our little Eton jackets, silk top hats, and 'slop bowl' collars. I had a swagger stick, and I think Fatty had another, and we were imagining that we were dashing young army officers. All of a sudden I heard a swishing noise. It kept up, and I could not think what it was. Fatty didn't seem to know. I noticed the crowd grinning, and I looked down and saw the brown paper coming out of Fatty's pant leg. Great was my humiliation. We had to stop and turn our backs to the crowd and get it out and get rid of it as best we could."

There were exciting days when Percy rode an old highwheeled bicycle, lent to him by a neighbor named Featherstone. "It was a rotten bike," according to the lad, but he went adventuring on it. He would ride to Athlone to watch the units of a British regiment in target practice on the shore of Lough Ree. Sometimes the soldiers took the youth to the barracks to show him guns and souvenirs and give him candy. It was then that he dreamed of becoming a lieutenant in the army so that he would have "the privilege of stopping bullets for Her Majesty the Queen."

Since the senior Magan had never known the meaning of work, his patrimony gradually slipped away. As political unrest swept over Ireland, landowners were threatened with loss of life and the confiscation of their property. When times grew more stringent for the father, he tended to make his son's existence a trying ordeal. What should be his vocation or profession? As to his training, Percy later said, "Our education was of the typical English sort. At the time I was sixteen, I had had five years of Latin and four of Greek, and had studied English literature but not much science."

Percy had no genuine interest in military things, so there was no point in preparing him for the army or navy. Neither was the master particularly enthusiastic about the lad's becoming a bishop in the church. However, since there was little choice, the father subjected his son to training under the supervision of a bishop of the Anglican

Church. Percy pumped the bellows of the organ and acted as an altar boy; but he had no enthusiasm for the church.

AN APPRENTICESHIP IN AMERICA

What should this distracted father do with his son who was seemingly a misfit? The boy, a student type of individual, had been schooled in hard circumstances and severe discipline; certainly he had not been pampered or spoiled. The master seemed always at odds with his energetic son. Percy had bitter memories of his last Christmas at Kilcreagh, for he wrote in later years: "That was a very miserable and a very unhappy Christmas for me. The master, against whom, however, I am thankful to say I bear no ill will, was determined I should have no part or thought in the presents and festivities, and I remember very well sitting halfway up the first flight of the stairs watching all of the rest of you, but the dear mistress couldn't stand it, and she came when the master was not looking and brought me down and got me into the ring a little bit at least. I shall never, as long as I live, forget her tender thoughtfulness. She had a wonderfully tender heart; and in those sad heart days that meant so much to me, the image of it all and her kind goodness has lain embedded in my poor old soul ever since, . . . and I am glad that I still cherish this sweet memory of Mother's unforgetfulness even although others may have felt that the earth would be better off without my presence."

About this time, while in Dublin, the father encountered a redheaded Irishman, Rotchford Edwards, who had crossed the Atlantic from America to recruit cheap labor for his farm near Red Cloud, Nebraska, and at the same time make a tidy sum of extra money. In colorful language he embroidered his stories of cattlemen making fortunes on the plains of Nebraska; and he promised that if Magan would pay him $650 to board and room the immigrant boy for two years, the farmer would make him a great cattleman. The bargain was completed, with the understanding in the senior Magan's mind that the sum would be deducted from the lad's rightful inheritance. Thus the master was relieved of the responsibility of rearing his teen-age son, and the youth was spurred to seek his fortune on the glamorous frontier of midwestern America.

Percy, sixteen and a half years old, bade a sorrowful farewell to his mother, sisters, and a little brother who was almost three years of age. Memories of the farewell flooded the mind of the man in later years when he described the scene photographically to his sister: "You were all standing on the steps of the limestone portico, as I was being loaded into the dogcart. I can remember how tall and stately the dear mother looked—bless her heart and memory; Shaen had lovely golden curls down his back, or at least over his shoulders. He was a very handsome child. The master and I were perched in front, and Din or John Mooney, I don't remember which, sat behind. Jimmy, the gray cob, acted as motor, and functioned pretty well at that. We drove out the back way by the little millrace (where we used to try to catch minnows) and to the 'short road' to Moate, and over the Galvan hill, while Mother pressed her forehead against the window of the red dressing room and watched till we were out of sight."

Percy and his father made the journey to Dublin together, and stayed overnight at the Shelbourne Hotel. In the lobby they met a Mrs. W. J. Quan, the wife of a wholesale merchant in Chicago, and her daughter Alice, who, upon hearing of the master's plan for his son, pleaded that the boy be spared from the lonely venture. However, the bargain had been made, and the stubborn Irishman paid the money for Percy's passage on the Cunard liner that was sailing for New York. When Mrs. Quan found that her pleas were in vain and that the boy would arrive in a strange country where he was friendless, she gave him letters of introduction to her husband in Chicago, and to her son-in-law, named O'Donahue, a tea merchant in New York City.

With a ticket in his pocket for passage on the steamship *Scythia,* the lad went alone to Cobh to begin his sea voyage. A contract for an apprenticeship and $64 were all his assets as he set out on this strange adventure. When young Percy mounted the rope ladder to the ship's deck in "dirty weather," his thoughts were divided between sadness and exuberance. He shrugged his shoulders and said to himself, "Well, anyway, I won't have to go to church anymore!"

AMERICA

On Tuesday morning, May 14, 1884, the *Scythia* docked in New York harbor, eleven days' sailing from Liverpool. On shipboard Percy had made the acquaintance of an officer of the Canadian government, and when the ship docked, the two young men clasped hands as they sang Stephen Foster's song, "Hard Times, Come Again No More." The Irish lad did not know a soul in all America; but after registering at the Westminster Hotel, near Sixteenth Street, he set out at a brisk walk on the streets of New York to find Mr.

Joseph J. O'Donahue, the tea and coffee merchant, whose office was near Wall Street.

Mr. O'Donahue was kind to this lad from his own country, and he saw to it that Percy was returned safely to the hotel in his private coach. The next morning the coachman took the lad from the hotel to the railroad station, where he boarded a train—with a seat in the parlor car—for Chicago. Arriving in the midwestern city, Magan went to the old Palmer House; and as a result of this contact, it was always his favorite hotel in Chicago.

After cleaning up from the dirty, tiresome trip, Percy started out to find Mr. Quan. He arrived at the home, 384 East Erie Street, in the evening, having made his way about the city riding on a horsecar and walking along muddy streets made passable here and there with sections of board sidewalks. The maid who came to the door was not inclined to welcome the strange boy; but after he had presented his letter of introduction, Mr. Quan welcomed him, and the visitor had an exciting evening with the family and several guests. The merchant offered Magan a position in his store; but the youth was determined to fulfill his apprenticeship contract. The experiences during the last five years, when his father had sent him off to school and forced him to sweat out his problems alone, were developing stamina and self-reliance in Percy. His tenacious Irish nature was asserting itself in a determination not to give up in a struggle.

WEST OF THE MISSISSIPPI RIVER

After spending a few days in Chicago, Percy began the last lap of his journey—a ride on a Burlington and Missouri Railroad train from Chicago to Red Cloud. The narrow, wooden, boxlike cars of the emigrant train had hard, reed-covered seats, a potbellied coal stove in one end to give a semblance of heat in cold weather, and dim oil lamps overhead that shed a dying glimmer of light at night as they swung dizzily back and forth. The Irish lad had discovered the magnificent distances of America on his trip between New York and Chicago; but now he would find even broader expanses as the slow train rolled westward. When the coaches were not crowded, passengers could put boards and cushions, which they rented from the newsboy, across double seats to form a hard, creaking bed.

The long train of baggage and passenger coaches crossed the Mississippi River and chuffed on into Iowa. Percy arrived at the Council Bluffs transfer station late the second afternoon of the journey. When he reached Omaha, a thriving town on the west bank of the Missouri River, he decided to go without his supper to save money.

That evening the only other passengers in the coach were a farmer's wife and her brood of children. As darkness fell, Percy became more and more lonely and his stomach grew more and more empty. When the mother brought out a basket of provisions to feed her flock, she told her eldest daughter to invite the lonely youth to eat with them. The girl approached Percy with the words, "Ma says, come and have a snack with us." "Snack" was a new word to the Irish lad, and he soon found, in this instance, at least, that it meant plenty of good food and cheerful companionship.

How that farmer's wife fed the gangling youngster! The "snack" included bread and butter with jelly and preserves, fried chicken, cookies, and fruit. As the hungry group ate the food, the woman questioned Percy, and he told her how he had come to leave home. Tears welled up in the woman's eyes, and she said, "Sonny, it doesn't seem right that your father should send you out to this strange country where you don't know a soul. It ain't right, it ain't right!" When it was time to sleep, Percy prepared his hard board for a bed, and the kind American mother placed a pillow under his head. She stooped down and kissed the homesick boy on the forehead as she said, "I wish, dear lad, that I could take you home with me; but I have so many in my own brood and so little room in our sod house."

Young Magan was touched by the kindness. Here on the broad plains of Nebraska was an expression of mother love the lad would never forget. How many times in later years he wished he might see this woman again! He often remarked that if they ever met in heaven, he would surely see his star in her crown!

ARRIVAL AT RED CLOUD

The next evening the train pulled into Red Cloud, a town of 2,500 inhabitants about a mile north of the Republican River. The Burlington and Missouri Railroad had built its main line between Denver and Kansas City through the valley in 1878. There was a red station, a roundhouse, a restaurant, and a hotel situated at the north end of the town; but the other business establishments were almost a mile to the south. Since no one was at the station to meet the immigrant boy, he probably stayed all night at the railroad's hotel.

Red Cloud, a frontier settlement only fourteen years old, had its beginning in 1870, when ranchers built a stockade to protect the westward-moving settlers from Indian raids. Land seekers and buffalo hunters stopped at the stockade to buy food, and in this way the town began to grow. The first hotel was constructed of logs and a sod roof, and homes were either dugouts (pioneer dwellings usually built in the side of a hill which gave warmth in winter as well as coolness in summer) or sod houses.

A young girl came with her family to Nebraska from Virginia in 1883, and moved to Red Cloud the following year, only a few months after Percy Magan arrived. She was Willa Cather, who would become a noted American novelist. In many of her books and short stories she described the coming of immigrant families—the Swedes, Germans, Bohemians, French, and Russians.

It was in this melting pot of Nebraska that Percy found himself alone and homesick on an April night in 1884. The following morning he took a look at the town, probably stopping at Miner Brothers' General Store. Willa Cather described Red Cloud as it no doubt looked to Magan. She wrote in *O Pioneers!* "The main street was a deeply rutted road, now frozen hard, which ran from the squat red railway station and the grain 'elevator' at the north of the town to the lumberyard and the horse pound at the south end. On either side of this road straggled two uneven rows of wooden buildings; the general merchandise stores, the two banks, the drugstore, the feed store, the saloon, the post office."

THE EDWARDS RANCH

Percy hired a horse and buggy at a livery stable to make the twelve-mile journey to the Edwards ranch. As the rig headed north across the rolling contours of the Republican Valley, the youth looked at the land, bare except for a few clumps of cottonwood trees. How strange was this country to eyes accustomed to green fields, neat hedges, and dense woodlands. Although he did not know it then, he was going to a ranch that was known as a "failure." Mildred Bennett declares that "Lord and Lady Edwards from Ireland" had "bought a ranch north of town, put up a rambling dwelling and advertised that they would teach young men of aristocratic European families how to ranch. Actually, the Edwardses knew nothing about farming, and their several young European protégés spent their time loafing in Red Cloud." If Percy could have read these lines in later years, he would have assured the writer that he was not one of the loafing apprentices!

When Percy arrived at the two-room frame house with a lean-to on the south side, set on a bleak, treeless farm, he was greeted by Mrs. Edwards and "two smelly children." There was also a servant girl who did the housework. Percy was shown to his quarters, which he could at least call a private retreat—an attic room with a cot, a rough board table, and a kerosene lamp. The stovepipe, running up from the kitchen stove through his room to the roof, gave welcome heat during the cold winter months; but it made the attic cell an oven on hot summer nights.

Percy soon found that Edwards had painted his property in rosy hues that were mere fantasy. Water for the house had to be drawn by hand from a deep well and carried three quarters of a mile. This was no fabulous cattle ranch; it was only a scrubby farm on a lonely prairie. The livestock consisted of a small herd of sheep, a few milk cows, and the farm horses. In later life, when he recounted his experience on the Nebraska farm, Percy wrote this to a relative in Ireland:

"I was the greenest little youngster when I first came to this country at the gallant age of sixteen that thee ever laid eyes on. I remember trying to make some biscuits, as they say in this country. I got the dough made, but had to squeeze it very tight in my hands to make it hang together. I did not know how to milk a cow, shear a sheep, or anything else. A friend of mine says I was so green that when I went out into the pasture, the cows were liable to eat me. Little by little I learned a few practical bits of knowledge, and I am sure that this experience will always make me more merciful to those who are coming along life's way."

The boy started his day at three-thirty in the morning, doing chores, milking the cows, cleaning the barn, harnessing the horses, and spreading fertilizer. "It was a part of my humble task in those hard days to lie out at night on the prairies with the sheep during lambing season with gun and dogs to keep the wolves away, and I have had the hair of my head frozen to the ground more than once so that the blooming wolf had an excellent chance to get away without some buckshot in his hide. I have had both feet frozen in my riding boots on the plains on three different occasions when trying to save Rotchford Edwards's cattle during winter blizzards while he was off filling himself with bad whiskey in the prairie village of Red Cloud."

A NEW VISION OF LIFE

After a year on the Edwards ranch, the youth decided it was time for him to leave. The rancher was indulging more and more in liquor; and when he became drunk, he was abusive to his family and to young Magan. Sometimes, too, the family would go off to town for several days, leaving all of the heavy work on Percy's young shoulders. Finally the seventeen-year-old boy received a letter from his father, giving him permission to cancel the contract and seek his own fortune elsewhere in the growing country.

Percy found work in Red Cloud at the home of Levi Moore, an elderly banker. The energetic youth did the chores, built the fires, worked in the garden, and ran errands for Mrs. Moore. The sympathetic couple were kind to the immigrant lad in his plight. When Edwards attempted to slur young Magan's character for canceling the contract, the banker's wife wrote a letter to the youth's mother, praising his character, industry, manners, and thoughtfulness. Taking advantage of Mr. Moore's invitation to enjoy the books in the well-stocked library, Percy delved into volumes of history in his spare time.

As the months passed, the lad made friends with a young couple, John Gross and his wife, who lived a few blocks from the Moore home. One Sunday, dressed in flannel shirt, work trousers, and boots, Percy dropped in for a visit, only to find the young wife dressed in her black silk skirt and white blouse, ready to go out. Percy inquired, "Where are you going?"

"To a tent meeting," said the wife. "There is a wonderful preacher holding services. Won't you come if my husband will agree to go?"

"There are no good preachers until they're dead and six feet underground," answered Percy skeptically, prejudiced by his background of formal religion. "I'd rather stay here."

"But," persisted the woman, "this preacher tells how the Bible prophecies are fulfilled in the history of nations."

These words caught the interest of the young student of history. Without showing too much eagerness, Percy said, "Well, if you will take me dressed as I am and walk up to the front of the tent with me, I'll go."

The husband and wife, joined by Percy, made their way to the tent, which was pitched on a vacant lot near the business center of Red Cloud. Two Seventh-day Adventist ministers, Elders L. A. Hoopes and G. E. Langdon, had begun a series of evangelistic meetings in the town on June 9, 1886. At this particular service the evangelist spoke on the prophecies of Daniel and the Revelation. The music was simple, and a young girl, Eliza Burleigh, played the small organ.

As the trio were returning home after the meeting, the young woman asked, "Well, Percy, how did you like the sermon?"

"I did not understand it, but I would do anything to become as good a preacher as that Reverend Hoopes. If I could be as good a man as that man, I would be willing to give up everything and go to saving souls as he does."

The next evening Percy was anxious to attend the tent meeting and hear the message of the evangelist. He finished his chores, got out his best suit and shirt, and rolled them in a neat bundle. Afraid that some of the young fellows in the town would see him and ridicule his church attendance, he went a roundabout way and dressed in the bushes not far from the tent. For two weeks he attended every service, and on July 4 he told Mr. Moore that he had decided to keep the Sabbath.

As Percy was hoeing potatoes in the Moore garden, he pondered over his relation to his family and particularly his father's attitude toward him. The boy seemed to hear a voice say, "Would you rather have your rightful inheritance from your father, or have an eternal home in heaven and an angel to guide you there?" During the months of absence from Ireland, Percy had written regularly to his mother. Now he informed her of his interest in religion and how he was learning to understand the doctrines of the Bible. When his father heard of the son's experience, he wrote him: "Since you have decided to make a fool of yourself, Percy, I have disinherited you. I never want to see your face again."

In the middle of the summer the meetings ended, with four persons baptized in the Republican River and accepted into church fellowship. Writing of the results of evangelism, Elder L. A. Hoopes stated in the *Review and Herald,* October 5, 1886: "A young man also accepted the message, who immediately commenced to carry the truth to others. He has decided to give his time wholly to the cause of the Master."

No doubt this young man was Percy Magan, for within two weeks after he was baptized he joined the evangelistic group, acted as tent master, went to work as a colporteur among his old friends, and, as his knowledge increased, gave Bible studies to interested listeners.

One evening he visited a family that lived in a crowded dugout. While Percy was studying with eight members of the family, a severe storm came up, and he was obliged to stay all night. The dugout had only a single room, but everyone was thankful for shelter. One by one the members of the family wrapped themselves in blankets and lay down on the floor, the men on one side of the room and the women on the other—feet to feet, leaving a narrow passageway between. The wind blew with hurricane force and torrents of rain came down amid crashing thunder and flashes of lightning. Early in the morning Percy arose and slipped out of the house. On his way back to town he stopped in a small clump of trees and removed his clothing. Here he spent an hour at an arduous but necessary task—picking off fleas!

The evangelists traveled from town to town through the southern part of the state, and reached Lincoln in time for the Nebraska camp meeting, September 15-21, where Percy heard stirring sermons by Elders S. N. Haskell and D. M. Canright. A Lincoln mission, begun the previous year by Elder G. B. Starr, gave the Irish youth an opportunity to continue his education. He worked and studied diligently until the spring of 1887. During that summer he went to Cambridge, Nebraska, with Elders Hoopes and J. E. James as caretaker of the evangelistic tent. One of his first tasks was to visit every house in the small town, soliciting subscriptions for the magazine, *Good Health,* an ordeal he sincerely disliked! The meetings ended abruptly one night when a tornado struck the town and tore the tent to shreds. The ministers left Cambridge for other duties, leaving the bewildered youth to clean up the mess and ship the salvaged equipment to Lincoln.

In the autumn Percy became a preacher in his own right, conducting meetings in a country schoolhouse near Grand Island, Nebraska. The attendance was fair, and several persons were baptized. But Percy realized that he needed more education, and his eyes turned east to the church college at Battle Creek.

2

Student and World Traveler

In 1888, Battle Creek, Michigan, was a quiet town of about 7,000 inhabitants. Settlers had originally come to the area because of the creek, which supplied power to operate sawmills, flour mills, a broom factory, and other industries. The first Seventh-day Adventist church in the community was organized in 1854 by Elders J. N. Loughborough and M. E. Cornell at the close of a series of evangelistic services held in a tent pitched at the corner of Van Buren and Tompkins Streets.

In 1855 the Adventists in Battle Creek were joined by those of other Michigan churches in a project to purchase land and pledge additional money to build a printing plant to publish the *Review and Herald* and other denominational literature.

Beginning in a small wooden building, the publishing house moved into a larger brick structure in 1861. The expansion of church activities called for more buildings, including offices for the General Conference and Mission Board.

When healthful living was recognized by the church leaders to be an integral part of Christianity, they decided to build a Health Reform Institute near the northwest outskirts of Battle Creek. The institution opened its doors in September, 1866, on the grounds where the Battle Creek Sanitarium would be erected twelve years later.

The growing Battle Creek church had many families with children and youth. Realizing the need for a distinctive system of Christian education, local leaders started the first Adventist school of any permanency in June, 1872, with Goodloe H. Bell as the teacher. Soon larger facilities were required, and on March 11, 1873, the General Conference voted to establish a college to train ministers. Cash and pledges totaling $54,000 were in hand for the enterprise when the construction of a college building was started on a campus across the street from the Health Institute. Battle Creek College opened its doors early in 1875, with Sidney Brownsberger as president. The enrollment increased during the succeeding years, the high mark of attendance being over 600 students.

Percy Magan heard of Battle Creek College through Nellie Rankin

Druillard, better known to hundreds of young people as "Aunt Nell," or "Mother D." This energetic woman, who was a teacher at the Lincoln mission school and later the treasurer of the Nebraska Conference, recognized the talent in the youth. She also noticed that he had a persistent cough, the result of too much exposure to the winter winds on the Edwards farm. Fearing that the cough might become chronic, Aunt Nell encouraged Percy to go to Battle Creek, where he could receive treatments at the sanitarium and also attend college.

The twenty-year-old Irishman, now accustomed to travel, arrived by train in Battle Creek at the Grand Trunk Station, on January 17, 1888. The crisp air of a Michigan winter morning caused Percy's ears to tingle as he walked up the streets lined with oak and maple trees, to find Battle Creek College. Mrs. Druillard had written her sister, Ida Rankin, preceptress and teacher at Battle Creek College, urging her to take a special interest in the newcomer.

DAYS IN COLLEGE

For some months Percy roomed with Ed Sutherland. Ed, the son of Joseph Sutherland and Mary Rankin—a sister of Ida and Nellie—had been reared on an Iowa farm. He worked in the college laundry to help pay his tuition and other expenses. In like manner, Percy's finances were in a precarious situation, and although he worked industriously at the Battle Creek Sanitarium as the operator of the rope-controlled elevator, he did not have enough funds to pay his tuition. Again Ida Rankin assisted Magan in continuing his education, by arranging for him to draw money from a trust fund that had been established by an elderly gentleman named Root. As he continued working at the sanitarium, he was promoted to more lucrative jobs until he became a patients' attendant and gained the notice of Dr. Kate Lindsay, the organizer of the Battle Creek training course for nurses.

College subjects, particularly Bible and history, delighted Percy, and he mastered them with ease.

Members of the college faculty also influenced Percy's thinking. There were W. W. Prescott, president; Uriah Smith, Bible teacher; and other men of sound scholarship. In late October, 1888, the youth attended the General Conference in Minneapolis. The spirit of the advent movement possessed him as he listened to stalwart leaders, such as Uriah Smith, S. N. Haskell, A. T. Jones, and E. J. Waggoner, and of course Ellen G. White. It was at the Minneapolis meeting that Percy heard Elders Jones and Waggoner propound the doctrine of righteousness by faith, and he accepted this vital Biblical truth as a part of his Christian philosophy.

When Percy entered Battle Creek College in January, 1888, Mrs. White was living in California, bringing to completion her work on the enlarged *Great Controversy*. When she attended the General Conference session of 1888, young Magan met her for the first time. He had, of course, heard a good deal about her and her work, and the White home at 303 West Main Street in Battle Creek had been pointed out to him. Following the meeting at Minneapolis, Mrs. White, early in November, returned to Battle Creek and lived there for the next ten months with those who assisted her in her work. It was not long before Mrs. White, learning of Percy's experience and needs, invited him to come and live in her home for a time. He was not slow in accepting this invitation.

The bashful youth was awed by Mrs. White. On the first morning when he came downstairs, Percy was greeted by the kindly woman. She said, "Good morning, lad, come near and let me see you. Did you have a good night's rest?" Then, smoothing his coat sleeve in her motherly way, she added, "That is nice cloth in your coat. I like nice wool, but I see there is a button off. Bring me my sewing basket, and I'll sew it on for you. Then we'll have breakfast and prayers, and you may go about your duties."

LEARNING DOCTRINES FROM ELLEN WHITE

Soon the mother love of Mrs. White won Percy's heart, a heart long starved for affection. While living in the White home, the youth developed his philosophy of religion. When Mrs. White explained the Bible doctrines, he realized that this world was a spectacle unto angels and unto men, a theater in which the conflict between good and evil had been waged for centuries. He realized, too, that man was a free moral agent who could choose right or wrong. These were important developments in the young man's thinking, for later he would understand and help others to grasp the fundamental doctrine of righteousness by faith, which Martin Luther had made a focal point in his religion. Percy learned the history of the advent movement—of how William Miller had studied the prophecies of Christ's return, how the believers in 1844 had been disappointed when Jesus did not come at the time they had set, and how ridicule, unbelief, and skepticism had broken up the group. Then out of that darkness there had arisen a new movement as a handful of believers met together and prayed for more light. They had studied the sanctuary of ancient Israel and had seen how it was an object lesson of the true sanctuary, or temple, in heaven.

The young man discussed with Ellen White the doctrines of the investigative judgment, the atonement, and the three angels' messages of Revelation 14. He caught a vision of the work the church must accomplish in order to fulfill the commission of Jesus Christ: "Go ye into all the world, and preach the gospel to every creature."

Young Magan understood the place of the spirit of prophecy among the Adventist believers. By the humble, consecrated life of the messenger, Ellen G. White, the church had been led step by step in its advance of the gospel. Throughout his life Percy Magan was true to his conviction that the church had received the divine prophetic gift. He received scores of letters from Mrs. White, counseling and directing his multitudinous activities in the fields of endeavor in which he was engaged, and he was always ready to accept their counsel.

Of his days in the White home, Percy had only happy memories. He remembered "with deep gratitude" the kindness of Mother White, and in letters he wrote her in later years, he frequently called her "Mother." In a letter to W. C. White shortly after Mrs. White's death, Percy wrote: "We shall all miss her very much indeed, and I shall greatly miss her, for a kinder or better friend I have never had. I often look back on the days in Battle Creek when we all lived at 303 West Main Street, and how kind she was to me."

When the General Conference Committee decided to send Elder Haskell on a round-the-world tour to survey strategic areas for mission stations, Mrs. White suggested that Percy would make an excellent traveling companion and secretary. She was anxious for the youth to visit his family in Ireland, and, if possible, establish better relations with his father.

Elder Haskell was amenable to the suggestion on condition that the young man would qualify to take his dictation, act as his valet, be a nurse if he should need treatments, and fill in as porter and guide. Percy grasped eagerly at the opportunity by taking shorthand from a former court reporter while mastering typing without any formal training. While in college, Percy had fallen desperately in love with a petite French girl who was also a student there. From her he learned a smattering of French, which helped him at times in

Europe. The thought of leaving her for a year-and-a-half trip abroad pulled at the young man's heart; but the girl promised to wait for him.

HASKELL GOES AHEAD

Elder Haskell sailed from New York on the steamship *Umbria,* Friday night, February 15, 1889, to attend meetings in England and northern Europe. Percy was to complete his year in college and join the minister in Europe later in the summer. There were conference sessions in the Scandinavian countries during March and April, which Elder Haskell, as well as Elder Olsen, the General Conference president, attended.

On the evening of July 17, 1889, young Magan left Battle Creek on the Michigan Central Express for New York City. The twenty-six-hour trip was uneventful, and after a day of sight-seeing in the metropolis he boarded the steamship *Etruria,* the fastest Cunard liner of that day.

About one week out of New York harbor the travelers sighted the cliffs of the west coast of Ireland. After passing Fasnet Rocks, the *Etruria* anchored in the Cove of Cork, where passengers for Ireland were taken ashore on a tender. Anxious to visit his home, Percy left the ship and boarded a train for Dublin. The passenger service was erratic, to say the least, for when the journey was about half completed, the engineer and fireman decided to quit work for the day. They left the train standing in a drizzling rain, and it was over an hour before railroad officials could find another crew to take the train on to Dublin.

For the first time in his life Percy was seeing Ireland through "American eyes." Now the country seemed small and provincial, the cities uninviting. He commented upon the backward methods of farming and the primitive modes of transportation. He visited his relatives at the old home, but he had little opportunity to enjoy himself, since the younger members of the family rode off on a hunt, leaving him with his father, who was coldly polite.

In London Percy met Elder W. A. Spicer, who had recently been made editor of the English *Present Truth.* Elder Haskell was at the time lecturing on Bible topics in that city. A diligent student of the Scriptures, the minister gave his secretary a postgraduate course in theology. However, it was not easy to be the secretary of an active, energetic man such as Elder Haskell. Percy had seven large suitcases and a typewriter to keep under his watchful eye. He was sometimes called from his sleep in the middle of the night to take dictation. Not content with generalizations, he delved into almanacs and histories to obtain the facts about various countries in order to give the Haskell articles valuable data and statistics. When checks were slow in coming from America to finance the travelers, the jack-of-all-trades secretary sometimes found temporary employment to raise sufficient money to see them through the emergency.

Early in August Elder Haskell and Percy sailed on the *Warwick Castle* for Cape Town. They traveled through Africa, across the Indian Ocean to Ceylon and India, and then on to China, Japan, and south to Australia. While Elder Haskell remained in Australia, Magan sailed for America on September 3 on the steamship *Mariposa,* visiting New Zealand ports, Samoa, and Hawaii en route.

When Magan walked down the gangplank in San Francisco, September 28, 1890, he had achieved the honor of being the first Seventh-day Adventist to complete a round-the-world tour for the church. He went at once to the camp meeting of the California Conference, which was being held in Oakland. According to the report of Elder Olsen, General Conference president, the young traveler brought "good news from afar" to the congregation. On the last afternoon of the session a foreign-mission service featured Percy Magan and the two young couples, Elders E. H. Gates and A. J. Reed and their wives, who were soon to sail on the newly constructed *Pitcairn,* which was dedicated the same day.

In the company of the General Conference president and Elders A. T. Jones and R. A. Underwood, Percy visited the Pacific Press Publishing Association at Twelfth and Castro Streets, Oakland, and the Rural Health Retreat at Saint Helena, in the beautiful Napa Valley. Percy made a comment about California which has held true through the years: "It is a glorious country—California—what a pity it is not larger, so that more of us poor Eastern mortals could live there!"

On October 8 the four men left Oakland by train for Oregon. At meetings in Portland on the following Sabbath and Sunday, Magan gave reports of the progress of the gospel in mission fields around the world. Since the Northwest needed a college where Adventist youth might be educated, plans were developing for the establishment of a school in the Walla Walla Valley. The four visitors accompanied the North Pacific Union Committee and the school board to Milton, Oregon, and Walla Walla, Washington, to survey possible sites for a college. Magan saw the Blalock farm, three miles from Walla Walla, which would soon become the campus of Walla Walla College.

The General Conference officials and Percy left the Northwest on October 15, traveling to Salt Lake City and on east through the Colorado Rockies and over the plains to Chicago. They arrived in Battle Creek on October 20. Percy could say of his trip: "We have traveled over 44,000 miles, and have taken a year, three months, three days, and an hour in which to accomplish the trip. By land and by sea we have been safely preserved to reach our home again."

The story of his round-the-world trip, recounted in colorful style, appeared as a series of forty-nine articles in *The Youth's Instructor* between January, 1890, and July, 1891.

He was anxious to see the petite French miss who had promised to wait for him. Indeed, he had purchased gifts for her in various lands he had visited! But alas, she had grown tired of waiting for her peripatetic lover and had turned her affections elsewhere. Percy's first experience in love ended with a sudden shock; but he philosophically declared, "At least I learned a smattering of conversational French in the experience!" Without further ado he distributed the presents to some of his friends. Among the gifts was a lovely hand-embroidered cashmere shawl, which he presented to Sally Sutherland. In later years she gave it to Percy's wife, who made it into a beautiful stole.

3

Marriage and a Profession

With his world travels behind him, twenty-two-year-old Magan was made assistant secretary of the General Conference Foreign Mission Board. Here began a lasting friendship with Elder W. C. White, the Board secretary, that was an inspiration to both men. In 1891, many mission reports and appeals signed with the initials P. T. M. were published in the pages of the *Review and Herald.* When calls for Bible instructors came from faraway lands, the assistant secretary urged Adventist young people who had been trained in denominational schools to dedicate their lives to mission service.

Percy also continued his studies at Battle Creek College, for he was determined to complete his course quickly and become a teacher. His experience as a secretary-reporter was now of special value to him, as he contributed series of articles to the church paper, and his name was listed among the regular writers for *The Youth's Instructor.*

During the Nineties the educational program of the church was in a state of flux. Ed Sutherland, who had received his B.S. degree at Battle Creek College in 1890, became the principal of the Minneapolis Academy that fall. In the spring of 1891 he was called to head the history department at Union College, Lincoln, Nebraska. During the summer vacation Magan joined his friend at Union College, and in July the two men attended the teachers' institute at Harbor Springs, near Petoskey, Michigan. A shift of faculty appointments took place during the summer, and Ed was invited to his alma mater as head of the history department and dean of men. Disappointed by the turn of events, he was ready to reject the offer of Battle Creek College until Percy reasoned with him.

Sutherland had not accepted fully the doctrine of righteousness by faith as it had been emphasized at and following the General Conference of 1888. But during these summer days his friend Magan showed him the beauty and reasonableness of this Bible truth. At this time, too, Magan, who had been influenced by Dr. Kellogg to accept a vegetarian diet as the best program for healthful living, convinced the Sutherlands that they should give up meat eating. Thus

Ed's dreams of vacation fishing in the Michigan lakes and enjoying the evening fish fries soon vanished.

The autumn of 1891 found the two men on the faculty of Battle Creek College. One year later Sutherland was called to be the pioneer president of the new school in the Northwest—Walla Walla College. When Battle Creek College opened in the autumn of 1892, Percy, while continuing his schoolwork, was listed officially as professor of Biblical history and literature. In 1895 he received the degree of Ph.B. from Battle Creek College.

As a serious pedagogue of twenty-five years, Magan took additional responsibilities upon his shoulders on June 14, 1892, when he married Ida May Bauer at the Bible Mission House at College Place, Chicago. The charming bride came from Kansas, having been born on a farm near Palermo, September 9, 1869. She had known the hardships of pioneer life in the Middle West, and after her family became Seventh-day Adventists, Ida, at the age of sixteen, left home to attend Battle Creek College. Devoted to her studies, the girl was graduated from the English course in 1890, a classmate of Sutherland. During college days she became acquainted with Percy, and the campus friendship culminated in marriage. The young couple went from Chicago to the bride's home on their honeymoon.

Returning, they rented a house in Battle Creek and set up housekeeping on the meager salary of an Adventist college professor, which was less than $5 a week! For ten years Percy was a member of the Battle Creek College faculty, teaching Bible, Biblical history, and world history, and also holding the office of academic dean.

A SOUND VIEW OF HISTORY

A classical education was emphasized at Battle Creek College from its opening in 1875 until Sutherland became president in 1897. The college bulletins of President W. W. Prescott's administration reveal the basic requirements of the classical course, which included five years of Latin and four of Greek. The scientific course called for five years of Latin, two of German, and one of Greek. Attempts were made between 1885 and 1893 to modify the program, but American education had built up such a tradition it could not be broken quickly even in an Adventist college.

When George W. Caviness was called to the presidency in 1894, he endeavored to maintain a high scholastic standing. However, by 1897, curriculum reform was under way and a "new order" was demanded. In an attempt to cast reflection upon the administration some men searched high and low for books—some owned privately by students or teachers—which had "anti-Christian" statements. With these supposed "exhibits" in front of them they demanded administrative changes. Finally a *coup d'etat* brought Sutherland to the presidency of the college.

In the light of this crusade for reform we can better understand Professor Magan's philosophy of history. During these years his views are revealed in several series of articles he wrote for the *Review and Herald* on the French Revolution, the relation of church and state, and other topics. He was anxious to correlate the study of history with Bible truth. To Mrs. White he wrote, "It is very clear to me, from the *Testimonies,* that history in connection with prophecy should have a large and important place in our schools; and not only in connection with prophecy, but also the history of the early Christian church and early events of a kindred nature." The emphasis upon a classical education had caused some of the teachers of Battle Creek College "to exalt books and authors" that did not "present the proper foundation for true education." The young Irish professor was perplexed as to the books that should be used for reference, since, as he said, "the large majority of historians are either indifferent, or else skeptics, or else infidels."

His sincere endeavor to present the philosophy of Christianity in his classes is explained in the same letter: "I have always called the attention of my classes to the objectionable passages, showed them the fallacy of these, and warned them faithfully against them. . . . I have never found (and I have watched with great care) that our students have ever imbibed any infidel ideas from the history work. . . . In fact, this is the only reason that we have in teaching history, *i.e.,* to teach the prophecies. I would not teach it for anything else unless it be to show what constitutes the rights of conscience and the proper sphere of civil government; and even these two phases, I suppose, might be included as parts of the prophecies."

In a letter to Professor W. W. Prescott, Magan described his methods of teaching, some of which may be considered "modern" in our day. He wrote: "If a student misses a recitation, that identical recitation has to be made up. If an examination is not satisfactory, that examination has to be done over again. The word 'star chamber' in the blank is a technical term which I have borrowed from English history to indicate a private examination. Very often now instead of having written examinations I take the students one by one, and give them from ten minutes to half an hour, according as circumstances may require, and in this way I find exactly what they know and what they do not know. It is to me very much more satisfactory than written examination work, though I think the latter has its place."

While reforms were essential in Christian education, yet there was great need for balanced judgment. Ellen G. White had repeatedly called attention to the Bible as the basic textbook. When Elder Jones said, "Make the Bible the basis of all educational endeavor," there were teachers and church leaders who accepted the statement literally. Some faculty members of Battle Creek College were ready to make the Bible the only textbook for courses in English, science, mathematics, and bookkeeping. However, the radical idea gave way to a sound viewpoint which set the Bible in the center of Christian philosophy and correlated its eternal truths with every subject.

THE NEED FOR VOCATIONAL TRAINING

Even before the Adventist Church began to establish a system of schools to teach its youth the essential principles and doctrines of Christianity along with secular subjects, Mrs. White had urged the denomination's educators to create a unique pattern of instruction, one that was different from that which was then popular in America. (See *Testimonies*, Vol. 3, pp. 131-160.) The hand as well as the mind should be trained. Schools should be located in rural areas, and vocational subjects should be linked with science, the liberal arts, and other formal studies.

When plans were shaping for the construction of a college in the vicinity of Battle Creek, Ellen and James White made trips through the surrounding country in search of possible sites. The Foster farm near Goguac Lake, five miles from town, was their first choice, with a forty-acre tract—the old fairgrounds—coming second. Either of these locations would have offered ample acreage for vocational training. However, in December, 1873, while the Whites were in the West, the church leaders purchased the Erastus Hussey estate of twelve acres on Washington Avenue in Battle Creek, directly opposite the sanitarium. It is reported that when Mrs. White heard of the action, "she wept bitterly."

When Sidney Brownsberger was installed as president of Battle Creek College in 1874, he declared that he knew nothing of industries and farming. Furthermore, the campus had been reduced to a scant seven acres when part of the land had been sold as lots to help defray the cost of construction. This gave little opportunity for the development of industrial and agricultural pursuits.

Under President W. W. Prescott (1885-94), the college developed its first vocational classes in carpentry, millinery, printing, cooking, household economics, and tentmaking. However, the program was accepted reluctantly by church members, and in 1887 the college stockholders urged that proper publicity on the industrial training be sent to Adventist homes, since some parents and students "felt a little inimical" to the plan. An article in the *Review and Herald* urged the church to "realize the great benefit to be derived from the manual training department and encourage the good work by every proper means."

As the college enrollment increased, the vocational facilities quickly became inadequate. Soon it was necessary to include dining and kitchen duties as well as the maintenance of the buildings in industrial training. However, there were weaknesses in the organization, and on March 22, 1889, a delegation of practical-minded women of the faculty appeared before the board and pleaded that the money expended on the vocational program be used in "home work and training."

On a Sunday afternoon two teams of students debated the vocational program, and their findings created a wave of popular interest on the campus. At the close of the college year (1889), the vocational program was liquidated, and the board voted "that no reference be made to manual training in the forthcoming catalog."

The next five years at Battle Creek College saw little industrial training. However, Christian education among Seventh-day Adventists was gaining momentum. In Australia, under Mrs. White's influence, the new Avondale School was being established with a strong vocational program. Then, too, depression days made it essential for the schools to offer work by which students could help defray their expenses. In this year the General Conference appointed a committee of eleven to study the aims and purposes of Christian education, and the report was given at the 1897 General Conference session in Lincoln, Nebraska. The survey showed that there was a need for abbreviated college courses that would quickly prepare young people for leadership in the church. There was a demand for elementary-school teachers and a call for the expansion of vocational courses.

Professor Sutherland, the president of Walla Walla College and one of the committee members, became vigorously enthusiastic about vocational training. In this same year he was installed as president of Battle Creek College, and he set as his goal the establishment of a "new order." That summer he received counsel from Mrs. White, in which she declared: "If one third of the time now occupied in the study of books, using the mental machinery, were occupied in learning lessons in regard to the right use of one's own physical powers, it would be much more after the Lord's order, and would elevate the labor question, placing it where idleness would be regarded as a departure from the Word and plans of God."

She said further: "There is a science in the use of the hand. In the cultivation of the soil, in building houses, in studying and planning various methods of labor, the brain must be exercised; and students can apply themselves to study to much better purpose when a portion of their time is devoted to physical taxation, wearying the muscles."

EDUCATION IN A NUTSHELL

Under the leadership of Sutherland and Magan, the college altered its course of study. The curriculum was made more flexible to enable students to select the subjects they desired. "The plan is known as the credit system," said Percy. "I am convinced that this is a step in the right direction." Early in 1898, short courses were introduced for mature students who were anxious to become missionaries as quickly as possible. President Sutherland announced in the *Review and Herald* of November 2, 1897, that the college administration intended "to provide a winter school of twelve weeks, complete in itself. Everything will be done to carry on this course so that it will be adapted to the needs of those who have good reasons for not spending more time in school." Then he listed the special groups to be trained: ministers, missionary workers, teachers, bookkeepers, and canvassers. This was to be an education in a nutshell!

The general reorganization of the college included the setting up of a new corporation, which was deliberately incorporated under the Michigan Benevolent Act in order to prohibit the college from conferring academic degrees.

Dean Magan remembered the industrial arts classes he had seen in successful operation in Africa and India, and he accepted the counsel of Ellen White concerning the place of vocational training in a college education. In 1881 she had presented counsel to the leaders in Battle Creek: "It would be well could there be connected with our college, land for cultivation and also workshops under the charge of men competent to instruct the students in the various departments of physical labor. Much is lost by a neglect to unite physical with mental taxation. The leisure hours of the students are often occupied with frivolous pleasures, which weaken physical, mental, and moral powers."

A PLAN FOR VOCATIONAL TRAINING

As Professors Sutherland and Magan surveyed the crowded conditions on the campus, they were convinced of the need to expand the industrial-education facilities. To dramatize the new program, the president got out a plow, Dean Magan drove the team, and 225-pound J. G. Lamson sat on the beam as they plowed the recreation grounds of the college and planted them to potatoes! In the summer of 1897 an eighty-acre farm, about a mile from the campus, was purchased.

The new property offered work for scores of students who had been raised in rural areas. Soon the administration was able to report that thirty acres of the property had been planted to fruit trees, shrubs, and berry vines, while the remaining fifty acres were prepared for truck gardening to supply food for the college kitchen.

From the time the school had been established, educators had been urged by Ellen G. White to include classes in practical homemaking for the girls as well as valuable industrial training for the young men; but the counsel had not been followed at Battle Creek College. Under the new regime, however, courses in tailoring for men and dressmaking for women were included in the program, and the sanitarium cooperated in buying the students' products. A broom factory and a printshop offered work that helped a number of students earn tuition and other expenses.

In the summer of 1899, Dean Magan reported on the progress of the industrial-arts program: "Our boys in the broom shop manufactured 3,000 dozen brooms, and we have found ready sale for these in the Chicago markets. We have some good friends there among the large wholesale merchants, who help us. Of course there is but little profit in the broom business; nevertheless, our shop cleared about $400 above expenses. We have also started a tailor shop, and several boys are learning the simple rudiments of that trade, so when they go to foreign fields they can make their own clothing. This shop made us a gain of $150 last year. We have been running a dressmaking department, but there was a loss of about $200. This came about on account of the one in charge not being really competent to make figures on goods, et cetera. We have found it exceedingly difficult to get someone who is competent to take charge of this work."

While President Sutherland concentrated his attention on the vocational program, Dean Magan guided the spiritual interests of the students and faculty. The greatest revival in the quarter century of Battle Creek College took place in the autumn of 1897. During the second week of November, the dean spoke in chapel on the theme, "The Spirit of God as the Great Means of Discipline." He endeavored to set forth God's love as it is portrayed in the Bible and the spirit of prophecy. The results of this week of dedication were remarkable. Through the last week of November there were prayer bands, testimony meetings, and personal interviews. The Friday-evening vesper hour found the chapel packed and all standing room occupied. This was the climax of the revival. On December 5 over ninety persons, most of them college students, were baptized at the Battle Creek Tabernacle. Percy Magan said, "Such scenes tender these hearts of ours, and teach us that the coming of the Lord is near."

Professor Magan's spiritual leadership had been recognized by the denomination before his thirtieth birthday, for on July 27, 1897, in the Tabernacle, he was ordained to the gospel ministry. Three of his close friends conducted the service—President Sutherland preached the sermon, W. C. White offered the ordination prayer, and A. T. Jones gave the charge to the new minister.

THE PROBLEMS INCREASE

Educational reform at Battle Creek did not come easily. There were opposition, bitter accusations, and lawsuits. Professor Magan declared that the philosophy of Christian education was "passing through an experience similar to that which was passed through in 1888 at Minneapolis, concerning the doctrine of righteousness by faith."

The college, located as it was across the street from the sanitarium, had not developed into a strong, independent educational institution. During the late Nineties the enrollment of the college "largely consisted of young people from the sanitarium. At one time there were in attendance at the college as many as one hundred students who were earning both their board and tuition by working at the sanitarium." Many of these students were actually enrolled in classes on the elementary level as a prerequisite to taking the nurses' course, while other young people were interested only in classes that fulfilled the entrance requirements of the American Medical Missionary College. The fundamental purpose of Battle Creek College—the training of Adventist ministers, evangelists, and missionaries—had been impaired by a slowness to launch into a broad program as envisioned in Ellen White's counsels, and it had been sidetracked because of the campus environment.

Sutherland and Magan realized that permanent reorganization was impossible as long as the college remained in Battle Creek. But what would happen if the school were moved? Looking back on the problem, Percy Magan later wrote: "It was quite generally predicted that instead of 'a new order of things,' the exodus from Battle Creek would mark the winding up of the school forever."

The failure of the college to meet the needs of the church was emphasized by Magan in a letter to Mrs. White: "The lines upon which the schoolwork was conducted for so many years, with the long Latin and Greek courses, have made the conferences somewhat afraid of us," he declared. "Those of us who are in the school now have to live down these prejudices, and they are not easily overcome. Then again, I do not think that these conferences appreciate the need of getting young men who have had Christian training in our school, into the ministry."

The dean revealed why the college should be moved to a new campus when he said: "God only knows, Sister White, the terrible odds we are working against in this place; God only knows the influences of the voices of criticism and scandal, calumny and misrepresentation which are made to militate against our work. The spiritual atmosphere here is anything but favorable for the training of even our best and most staunch young men and women for the work. . . . They know the desire there is on the part of many, even of the church members, to have the old order of things restored and to have infidel and pagan textbooks put back into the schools."

Bicycles were a popular mode of transportation in those days, and the two college administrators sometimes loaded their vehicles in the baggage car of the train, got off at some Michigan town, and rode through the country, where they saw ideal campus sites in rich farming areas. Within a year after he became president, Sutherland was urging Mrs. White to use her influence to relocate the college. She recognized the impetuousness of youth, for she later said of President Sutherland, "He is young; but this is in his favor." Without discouraging the vision of Magan and Sutherland, she urged them to be patient and move deliberately. In a letter addressed to both men in 1900, Mrs. White said, "Nothing in regard to disposition of school property should be engaged in . . . at the present time. . . . Everything is to be carefully studied and prayerfully considered from cause to effect. . . . When your school interests should be transferred, it will be at a time that will not mean defeat, but victory."

Before the college could be moved it would be necessary to formulate a plan to pay off the debt of over $80,000. For years Ellen White had expressed deep concern about the finances of the schools. The charge to students, $17.50 a month for tuition, board, and room, was too low to meet operating costs. Furthermore, the management of the institution had continued to erect new buildings and expand facilities without having sufficient funds in the bank to cover the costs.

A PLAN TO CLEAR THE SCHOOLS OF DEBT

In 1898, Mrs. White, who was living in Australia, proposed that a new book then in preparation be used in a sales program to pay the debts of the school. "In order to help in this cause, I have proposed giving my book on the parables [*Christ's Object Lessons*]. I feel very anxious that the General Conference shall act unselfishly in regard to this book, which is to be published to help the schools."

Mrs. White donated the book, including all royalty and the work of her stenographers and helpers. The two publishing houses, the Review and Herald and the Pacific Press, agreed to print 300,000 copies of the book without charge for the labor. Gifts poured in to cover the cost of illustrations, paper, typesetting, and binding materials.

Professor Magan was elected secretary of the committee to promote the distribution and sale of *Christ's Object Lessons* among the churches, and he went to New York to arrange for an illustrator to do the art work. In 1900 he became the executive officer of the program, while carrying on his college duties as academic dean and professor of history. In December, 1900, and January, 1901, he visited churches in Oklahoma, Texas, and Colorado for the Relief of Our Schools Project.

The fund-raising program continued into 1902; and when Professor Magan became dean of the new college at Berrien Springs, Michigan, all of the detail work continued to pass through his office. His secretary, Mary Cook (later Dr. Mary McReynolds), recounted the tremendous task that confronted them. "We sent out as many as 1,200 circular letters at a time. To each church were sent a specific number of books to be sold by each church member. I remember very well on one occasion I had a heavy run of circular letters to be gotten out, and all the envelopes were addressed by hand. Those letters had to be in the mail the following morning. I went to the Orinoka Hotel, where the students were being housed, and asked the preceptress for permission to get help from the students. It was the night for prayer meeting, but she told me I might have anybody who had not gone to the service. I went upstairs and knocked on the door from which came the sound of many boys' voices. There were six or seven of the boys in one room, occupied in ordinary conversation. They all responded to my request, followed me back to the offices, and worked until after midnight addressing envelopes. That batch of circular letters went out to the churches on time in the morning mail!"

A heavy winter snow did not chill the ardor of the collegians, for Dean Magan's secretary said, "We waded into snow knee-deep, going to all the homes in Berrien Springs, and within the next week every house within a hundred miles of Berrien Springs had been visited. In fact, most of them had been visited from one to three times!"

Professor Magan sold twenty-five copies of *Christ's Object Lessons* to a wealthy businessman. When the educator had carried the last ten books upstairs and placed them on the donor's desk, Percy's thrift got the better of him. "What are you going to do with all of these?" he asked. "You only need one copy for yourself."

"I don't really know," confessed the businessman.

"Let me take them back and sell them again," suggested the promoter, pocketing the money.

When the man consented, the Irish educator, his eyes sparkling, went down the stairs with twenty-four books and the full $25!

This project required a combination of organization, money-raising, and colporteur work. Magan said with a smile, "When I was converted and joined the church, I told the Lord I'd do anything but sell books and raise money. But do you know, it seems that is what I have been doing most of the time ever since!"

MOVING THE COLLEGE FROM BATTLE CREEK

The year 1901 was momentous for the educational program of Seventh-day Adventists. On the morning of April 12, during the

General Conference session at Battle Creek, Percy was awakened early by a call from Mrs. White. A few months earlier she had returned from Australia to the United States and had made her home in Northern California. During this conference session she was staying as a guest at the home of Dr. J. H. Kellogg. As Percy recalled the interview, he told of how about half past five in the morning one of the workers came over and said Sister White wanted to see him. He dressed as fast as he could. At six o'clock he was with her. She asked him if he remembered when he and Professor Sutherland had through correspondence discussed the moving of the college out of Battle Creek. "I told you at the time," she said, "not to do it. Now I am ready to tell you to do it. What we will do with the old plant I do not know. I think possibly we may be able to sell it to the sanitarium. I do not think even then that we will be able to realize enough to pay off anything on the principal. Perhaps we will get enough to pay its debts. We will have to go out single-handed—empty-handed. It is time to get out now, for great things will soon be happening in Battle Creek."

At the nine-o'clock session Magan made his report on the sale of *Christ's Object Lessons* and the program of school debt reduction. At the close of the report, Mrs. White arose and challenged the conference to action as she said, "The school, although it will mean a fewer number of students, should be moved out of Battle Creek. Get an extensive tract of land, and there begin the work which I entreated should be commenced before our school was established here—to get out of the cities, to a place where the students would not see things to remark upon and criticize, where they would not see the wayward course of this one and that one, but would settle down to diligent study."

Paying special tribute to the two college administrators, she declared, "Changes will have to be made. But it is hard to break away from old habits and practices; and there are those who have felt inclined stubbornly to resist everything in this line. I am glad to say that Brother Magan and Brother Sutherland have made advancement in reform. . . . You are not to think that you have made a failure in the school." The two educators were urged to "go forward in the name of the Lord God of Israel . . . to educate young men and women."

On the same day the Seventh-day Adventist Educational Society, which was actually the constituency of Battle Creek College, voted to approve the move of the college from Battle Creek. Four days later the Michigan Sanitarium and Benevolent Association, which was the constituency of the sanitarium, voted to purchase the college buildings for $108,000 to house the American Medical Missionary College and the Sanitarium Training School for Missionary Nurses, which had over 120 medical students and 300 nurses without suitable classrooms, laboratories, or dormitories.

When the conference ended on April 23, two happy college administrators plunged into the task of making their dream come true. The money from the sale of the college would pay off all debts and leave some $26,000 to apply on the new school. Of course, there was one hitch in the plan—the money to pay for the college buildings would have to be raised by the sanitarium constituency!

Nevertheless, like Caleb and Joshua of old, Sutherland and Magan set out to conquer the "promised land." "This new school," wrote Magan to Mrs. White, "must be the Avondale of America. We must make it the light set upon a hill." They, along with several other faculty members, were anxious to make the new college self-supporting. They saw the General Conference Association burdened with hundreds of thousands of dollars indebtedness created by institutional expansion without proper financial provision to meet the obligation. They desired the school plant to be owned by the church organization and the program to be under the direction of the General Conference; but what they had in their hearts they had declared earlier: "We feel that God has called upon us to set an example to our brethren by working on a self-supporting basis ourselves; and we have faith, good heart, and courage to do this."

Although it was already the first of May, these men were determined to find a suitable campus, move all the college equipment, provide housing for faculty and students, and begin classes in the autumn of the same year! It was a stupendous task; and only a Sutherland and a Magan would have believed it could be done!

4

Establishing a New College

Life has a thousand separate threads, and it is often difficult to weave them into a tapestry of achievement; yet sometimes the varicolored strands do work themselves into a unique pattern. Such was the experience of Percy Magan, trailblazer for Christian education.

The concept of the new Seventh-day Adventist college was given impetus by Mrs. S. M. I. Henry, a national evangelist of the Woman's Christian Temperance Union. In 1896 she went to the Battle Creek Sanitarium as a patient. As the result of an experience in which she was healed in response to prayer, and through Bible studies given her by Professor Magan, she became an ardent Seventh-day Adventist. Particularly through her writings and counsel she made a valuable contribution to the wives and mothers of the church.

When Mrs. Henry heard that the college administrators were searching for a new campus where a college could be located, she introduced Magan and Sutherland to a group of civic-minded persons in Berrien Springs, before whom she had given a temperance lecture. Interested in starting a school to be called the People's University, this group of Christian socialists had found an ideal site for a college—a 272-acre farm near the village of Berrien Springs. When those sponsoring the university were unable to carry out their dream, they willingly gave their option for the land to the educators.

In later years Dean Magan described his reactions when for the first time he viewed the proposed campus. He wrote: "It was a lovely day in the month of May, 1901, when two tired men stacked their bicycles under the beautiful old maple trees which lined a spot by the road on that plot of land which we then knew as the Garland farm. It was not far distant from the bluff which overlooked the dark waters of the Saint Joseph River, and the flat lands extending to the left, then classified as the Richardson farm. These men had ridden their bicycles from South Bend, Indiana, through deep sand and dust, on the narrow, hilly roads which connected South Bend with Niles and Berrien Springs. There was no pavement in those days, and the only means of crossing the Saint Joseph River was by a hand-powered ferry, following which about two miles more of sandy road had brought the travelers to the Garland farm."

A NEW SITE IS PURCHASED

To the dusty explorers, the old vineyard was a dream. It seemed quiet and peaceful, a haven of rest away from the turmoil and internecine warfare of Battle Creek at that time.

Ed Garland agreed to honor the option until the administrators could present the proposition to the college board. After the board voted to purchase the property, Magan wrote a description of it to Ellen White. "At the morning meeting [July 16, 1901] it was voted to purchase the improved farm, viz., the Garland property, and unimproved farm, viz., the Richardson property, and the piece of woods. This was really a little more land than we felt was best to get, but the way the land lay and the way the watercourse lay, we felt it was the very best thing we could do. There are 106 acres in the Garland place, 110 in the Richardson place, and about 40 acres in the grove, making all told 256 acres, or, cutting out the grove, 216 acres. . . . The fruit farm will yield an immense income, and is in such beautiful condition now that it will be an inspiration to our students to keep it in the same condition as it comes to them. The Richardson farm will furnish a fine opportunity to make good land out of poor and rundown land, and the piece of woods will always be a magnificent place in which to hold our summer sessions of the General Conference, or to hold a camp meeting, or for the purpose of educational assemblies. The magnificent bluffs overlooking the beautiful river speak only of nature and of nature's God. A more quiet and peaceful and beautiful spot I have never seen."

Concerning the site for the college, Mrs. White declared, "I am much pleased with the description of this place. . . . In such a place as Berrien Springs the school can be made an object lesson, and I hope that no one will interpose to prevent the carrying forward of this work."

When it was known in Battle Creek that the college was to be moved to Berrien Springs, there was no rejoicing among the church members. Magan remembered that "there was no kindly farewell for us when we left. There were no speeches, nor dinners, nor the like. Battle Creek, and many of the well-known professors of the day, did not want to see the school moved."

Faced with opposition, lack of money, a divided faculty, and no college buildings, Sutherland and Magan went forward by faith. "If there ever was an institution born without a golden spoon in its mouth, it certainly is the Berrien Springs school," said Dr. David Paulson, after he realistically surveyed the grounds for the college.

Bringing the new college into existence required more than the board's approval of the purchase of a farm and the moving of the equipment; money was essential. Magan later declared of the pioneering venture, "We did not own as much as one foot of land at Berrien Springs, and I did not own as much as my own home at that time." Therefore, Magan and C. M. Christiansen went to the Farmer's Bank in Battle Creek and borrowed $3,000 over their own signatures in order to have the necessary cash to pack and ship the college equipment to Berrien Springs. Money from donors totaled over $7,000, which helped to make the first payments on the land.

Shortly after mid-July the dean accompanied sixteen bulging freight cars of books, laboratory equipment, furniture, and supplies to Berrien Springs. The cars sat on the siding near Main Street for several days until the location of the temporary quarters for the college and students was determined. Possession of the farm could not be obtained until the purchase price had been paid, and not until autumn would the money from the sale of the Battle Creek property be forthcoming. Furthermore, there were no buildings on the new campus except a farmhouse and one or two tenant houses. Therefore, temporary buildings were essential if a school was to operate in 1901-02.

Since the county seat had been moved from the village to Saint Joseph, the citizens of Berrien Springs offered the vacant courthouse to the administration. The former quarters of the probate judge, registrar of deeds, and county clerk made offices; and the old Orinoka Hotel, with some forty inexpensive stoves to add a semblance of warmth to the rooms, became the dormitory.

The contents of the freight cars were finally unloaded in rooms in the courthouse and jail, but the inventory of supplies to establish a college was amazingly meager. The supplies included: fifty cots, fifty bedsteads, springs, mattresses, bedding, tablecloths, towels, small tables, dishes, kitchen utensils, stoves, saws, axes, hatchets, laundry tubs and washboards, a team of horses, a wagon, lamps, oilcans, spades, a piano, commodes, bureaus, a carpet, books, a wheelbarrow, and a map of the mission stations of the world.

Emmanuel Missionary College was the name suggested by Homer

R. Salisbury, faculty member; and when it was officially accepted, Dean Magan said it symbolized the development of the new school, for every experience proclaimed, "God with us!"

STUDENTS IN JAIL

When college opened, it could truthfully be said that the students were behind bars, for the classrooms were twenty renovated jail cells! Magan's office had connotations of discipline, since it had once been the sheriff's office. The dean often said facetiously, "The place to begin an educational reform is in a jail!" The families of faculty members found temporary homes as best they could in the village of Berrien Springs. As business manager and dean of the college, director of construction of new buildings, promoter of the Relief of the Schools program, and educational secretary of the General Conference, Magan could truthfully say, "I am doing five men's work."

In a systematic way he laid the groundwork for a well-planned institution. "I have surveyors at work now making complete maps of the entire 'Emmanuel College' estate," the dean explained to W. C. White. "We are also making plotted plans of what will be the campus and building site. These will be on a large scale and will show the land in bird's-eye and profile forms. I will endeavor to obtain for you a map of southwestern Michigan, showing railways, rivers, and location of the school. I am having photographs made of the most interesting spots on the farm: the river, the bluff, the vineyards, the woods, and also the old courthouse buildings."

The industrial program was put into effect immediately because of the need for student labor on the new buildings. To the administrators Mrs. White wrote, stressing the vocational program. The contents of the course of study were also to be unique, for Mrs. White declared the educators should introduce "into their model school only those books and methods of teaching that they thought would help the students to form symmetrical characters and to become useful workers in the cause." In this pioneer effort they were to make "sweeping strides" in "the right direction."

By the summer of 1902 only one major school building was ready for occupancy. Magan reported the progress in these words: "Our Manual Arts building is completed. It is about sixty-two by thirty-four feet, with a fine basement; two stories above and a garret. We are at present using the basement for our dining room and kitchen, and are feeding in the neighborhood of 175 to 200 people. The first floor contains our store and carpenter shop. We have two rooms for the store, in one of which we keep general provisions for the kitchen department, teachers, and others employed on the premises. In the other room we keep our supplies of nails; builders' hardware; tools, for sale for the boys; locks, hoes, in fact, everything that we need on the premises. . . .

"Our shop is doing very well. We buy our stuff and make up our own window casings and everything of that sort, instead of buying them from the regular mills. We have no power machinery, but have several pieces of hand machinery which have stood us in good part through the summer. . . .

"Professor Sutherland's house is finished, and he is living in it. Another cottage, which was originally designed for me to live in, is also nearing completion, and will soon be ready for occupancy. . . .

"The large brick basement of the Domestic Arts building is finished, and by Friday evening the frame will have been raised. We are also laying the stone foundations for the Study Hall building. If our money was only coming faster than it is, we could push things more rapidly, but with our law that we will not go in debt a penny, we are sometimes delayed on account of means."

The first buildings on the new campus were largely flimsy, vacation-type cottages and an octagonal auditorium, named Memorial Hall, in "remembrance of God's goodness" in establishing a school in the country. The money for the hall was donated by Ida Magan, her entire patrimony.

Although the business manager, C. M. Christiansen, had wanted to build substantially with bricks manufactured in a campus kiln, President Sutherland would have none of this. He demanded austere wooden buildings with no thought of beauty or architecture. "We want our buildings to be simple and small, without heat and electricity, for that is the kind of buildings our students will find in the mission fields," said the president. "There must be no one large and handsome building, nor must the buildings be erected on the ordinary quadrangular plan, but on a meandering line in order to get plenty of fresh air and sunshine. Furthermore, such an arrangement will discourage the growth of pride and institutional spirit."

When the college year began in 1903, there were some three hundred persons—students, teachers, and their families—on the campus. Three large homes (seven to nine rooms each) had been completed and occupied by teachers. The girls lived in the attic of the Domestic

Arts building, while the boys were housed in "attics and various corners" of other buildings.

That winter was critical for the college, since it faced a stringent period of finance so desperate that it was difficult to pay the teachers. Students also endured hardships and inconveniences in their living quarters. "We have no well, not even a bathtub," said the dean. "Our students bear these things with great fortitude and Christian courage, but it distresses me beyond measure, especially when I know that some of them are suffering from lack of these facilities. When our poor boys and girls get sick it pains me deeply, we are so poorly equipped to give them proper attention and to take care of them."

The students pioneered in every type of construction, as the dean reported to A. G. Daniells: "This is Thanksgiving and a most beautiful day. . . . Our boys are setting up the furnaces and doing the tinner's work at the Study Hall building. No mechanic except one mason has struck a blow on this entire building. The installation of the heating plant was a new experience to the boys, but they have gone at it with good courage and have done splendidly. We have as fine a class of young ministers, who are also capable, self-reliant, commonsense men, as I have ever seen anywhere in my life." Even so, there were mistakes in construction. It might be mentioned, for example, that the Domestic Arts building, when finished, was twenty-two inches narrower at one end than at the other!

The organization of the curriculum, the details of the campaign to relieve the school of debt, and a thousand decisions concerning the new buildings, rested on the dean's shoulders. Also to this clever Irishman fell the lot of soliciting businessmen for donations to assist the growth of the institution, and he thoroughly enjoyed this assignment. However, the organization of the school suffered because of the frequent and prolonged absences of Sutherland and Magan.

In the dean's office there was thrift and precision. Mary Cook, Professor Magan's secretary during the first year of the new college, declared that he had five grades of stationery for his correspondence. The most expensive was for top business and railroad executives; the second, for General Conference officials; the third, for union conference leaders; the fourth for "lesser lights"; the cheapest, for ordinary folks. "And woe to the secretary who put a letter on the wrong stationery!" she added. The letters that went from the office could have no striking over of a "c" to make an "e." The page would be done again and again until it was correct, for erasures were not tolerated.

Since office equipment was needed in every department, the dean solicited various firms in Chicago for gifts. The best quarter-sawed oak files, desks, chairs, and tables were given to the college as the result of his contacts. One day he walked into a large manufacturing plant, met the president, and described the purpose and needs of Emmanuel Missionary College, with special emphasis upon the industrial-arts program, which required the best equipment to train students. Within a few days the latest model Miehle press arrived on the campus for the printshop, a gift of this manufacturing company.

PROVIDENTIAL LEADINGS IN THE GROWING COLLEGE

With the dean's efficiency was mingled a deep love and tenderness for God's work. When funds for the construction of the Advocate Building were exhausted, President Sutherland made plans to solicit donations in the Northwest. However, the school did not have the money for him to make the railroad trip to visit prospective donors. One Friday morning the president and the dean went to Chicago. Upon their arrival at the railroad station waiting room, Magan left the president sitting on a hard bench while he went to the superintendent's office. "Ed, you stay here and pray," Magan had admonished his colleague, "even if it takes me the rest of the day."

When the dean entered the office of the railroad executive, he noticed that the man at the desk was pale and his hands were trembling. In his kindly way, the educator said, "You are in sorrow, perhaps? Tell me about it."

The businessman spent the next hour recounting the sad experiences that had come to his family—the death of two daughters and the serious illness of his wife. After they had talked as friends, the superintendent suddenly said, "But this is not what you came to hear. What can I do for you?"

Before stating his business the sympathetic educator spoke of God's love and of the willingness of the Father to bear man's burdens and griefs. Afterward he told the gentleman of the needs of the college, and how the building program could not continue unless the president obtained donations from interested parties in the Northwest. He admitted that President Sutherland needed a railroad ticket! The understanding superintendent signed a paper, Magan hurried to another office, and soon he rushed back to the waiting president with tickets for five separate trips to places where donations might be obtained. The president caught the afternoon train!

That evening, back on the college campus, the dean spoke to the student body at the vesper hour service held in the half-completed chapel. As he recounted God's providential guidance in the experiences of the day and read the promises of more abundant blessings to come, the young people took courage and gave expression to their faith in a thrilling hour of dedication.

REFORM WAS NOT MERELY A THEORY

In addition to the complex problem of carving a college campus out of a Michigan farm, the administrators faced many discouraging moments. Since the president and the dean were young, it was easy for those with years of experience to criticize the efforts of youthful faculty members. At a college board session in October, 1901, only a few months after moving the college from Battle Creek, some members proposed that Elder W. W. Prescott be elected president because Sutherland was "young and inexperienced" (although he had been president of three colleges). The dean came to the defense of the administration. "Educational reform has not been a mere theory with us," he explained. "We have had to grapple with hard and difficult questions such as the textbook question, getting the college out of Battle Creek, inaugurating, starting, and organizing the church-school work. . . . We will gladly cooperate in any way that we can, but do not feel that we should be asked to bear the responsibility of guiding the school if it is necessary for someone to come in to make a decided change in the essential things of the school, such as the proper principles of teaching from the Bible."

Ellen White also defended the work of Sutherland and Magan, when she said, "There are those who with the Bible as their standard have been working in the fear of the Lord to carry out the principles of true education. They are not old men, but they are, nevertheless, men whom the Lord desires to place on vantage ground. . . . But as they have tried to carry forward the work, their efforts have been criticized, and the question raised, Should not older teachers be brought in to take the burden of this work? . . . The Lord encouraged these brethren, giving them victories that taught them valuable lessons and strengthened their confidence. It is not according to His plan for some other worker to come in and take the burden of this work upon his shoulders, supposing that he can do a much better and larger work. This is not right."

During these busy years when Magan was carrying heavy responsibilities, his personal diaries reveal no discouragement and no bitterness over the attacks that were made on the college administration. The source of his spiritual strength is revealed in such entries as "Prayed and read the Bible," "Prayed in my study," "Spent the forenoon over on the far bluff praying," "Sat in study reading my Bible."

As a diligent Bible student, the man delved into the lessons of Holy Scripture and applied them to his own personal need. He once said: "I rejoiced in the thought that if others criticize me, it is because their criticism will be a blessing to me. If the things which are said are true, as I humbly accept them, my disposition will be changed, and I will become a more effective servant of Jesus Christ. If the things which are said are not true, by accepting them in the sweet spirit of the Master, they will only adorn one's disposition, and help to fit one for a greater place of usefulness in God's work. I have always believed that God will not ask us, when we come before the judgment bar, how much the other fellow has abused us, but that the question will be, 'How sweet have you kept under it?' I know that God called me to this work, and no amount of criticism, just or unjust, shall ever drive me out of it. There are certain principles which I believe are right, and which at present are being trodden underfoot and ignored, and I have absolute confidence in God that, in spite of my clumsy, inefficient way of standing for these principles, He will yet cause them to triumph, and cause me to triumph with them."

5

Through Joys and Sorrows

Battle Creek was known in Adventist circles from the day in 1853 when James White visited the village and told the small group of believers, not yet organized into a church, "I am much impressed that if you are all faithful, there will be quite a company in Battle Creek." Certainly the impression was fulfilled! The town grew, and so did the Seventh-day Adventist denomination. The first church building in Battle Creek was an 18 x 24-foot structure erected in 1855 on Cass Street. The first building to house the printing equipment used in printing the *Review and Herald, The Youth's Instructor,* and pamphlets and books was erected the same year. The west side of Battle Creek had a building boom during the next twenty years, when the sanitarium and college were established and these institutions and the General Conference required housing for their personnel. In 1879 the original Tabernacle, which saw many a conference and council session, was dedicated; but by 1895 its 3,000 seats could not hold the Sabbath congregations.

The town was a hive of activity in 1892, largely as the result of the many health-food factories that were springing up. Soon Adventists were speculating in "land and food propositions," and there were numerous unwise business ventures. A decade later Magan could say, "The town of Battle Creek has come to be known throughout the whole central and eastern states as 'the Adventist mining camp,' in fact, these very words were used by businessmen from New York who came into Battle Creek the other day."

Late in the summer of 1892, after their honeymoon in Kansas, the Magans arrived in Battle Creek, rented a small house, and furnished it with careful thrift. Marriage brought to Percy the security and affection he had not known since early childhood. The couple were undaunted by sacrifices, for the young husband had known only hardship and privation since the day he left Ireland, and Ida had developed the pioneer spirit on the Kansas farm. It was well that they did not expect many material blessings during those early years of marriage, for times were hard. The bank panic of 1893 and the depression that followed were felt in every city and hamlet of the nation.

On August 7, 1893, a boy was born to the Magans, and the lusty youngster was duly named Wellesley Percy. The growing child was assured a playmate, when a little over three years later, on September 24, 1896, a second boy, Shaen Saurin, was born. He was given the Irish name in honor of Percy's younger brother.

MOVING TO BERRIEN SPRINGS

If life was busy for the Magans in Battle Creek, its tempo increased when they moved to Berrien Springs. After the year in temporary quarters in the village, Percy and Ida, with their two sons, moved into a modest new home, called "Shamrock," on the college campus. The man of the house had the task of landscaping the yard; and the spring and summer mornings found him up at four or five o'clock, working in the strawberries, hoeing potatoes, chopping wood, or carrying the water. This was a strenuous program for the dean, since he had suffered a severe attack of typhoid fever about a year before the move from Battle Creek. It had been a protracted siege which sapped his energy; and, in 1901, in his weakened condition, he suffered a relapse which left him with myocardial complications.

As the result of the fever Percy lost most of his hair, with the handsome pompadour which is seen in his early photographs. The bout with typhoid fever had also been a strain upon his wife, since she had nursed her sick husband for weeks. Ellen White paid special tribute to the devotion of Ida Magan when she said, "Sister Magan worked with her husband, struggling and praying that he might be sustained. . . . She strove untiringly to maintain a perfect home government, teaching and educating her children in the fear of God. Twice she had to nurse her husband through an attack of fever."

Rigid economy on a denominational wage was a prime essential, particularly when there were two growing Magan boys to clothe and feed. In December, when the going was particularly hard, Percy had unburdened his heart in a handwritten letter to Mrs. White. He said, "I am so weak after the fever that if I can get enough money together I will go to Los Angeles for a couple of months. My wife's parents have a farm near there. My nerves are pretty shaky, and while I am picking up quite fast on the whole, I feel far from strong.

"I cannot bear the thought of leaving the work at Berrien Springs so long. Professor Sutherland cannot, I fear, stand the strain much longer. He is working far beyond his strength. Now that I am gone there is no business manager at the school at all. There is no one to plan for the buildings; to see to getting the money, or to look after their erection."

In reply, the sympathetic Ellen White wrote to Percy, "My brother, I am deeply sorry for you and your family. . . . Be not concerned in regard to your wages. God will not leave you without some help and comfort for yourself, your wife, and little ones."

Let it be said that in the diaries of Percy Magan there are no statements of bitterness or complaint concerning personal finances; and in the grueling pace of these years, he seldom refers to weariness except after a serious illness. Many weeks out of the year Magan traveled in the interests of the school. Berrien Springs could not be reached easily by public transportation, and a horse and buggy in summer, or a sleigh in winter, was necessary to get the dean to the Michigan Central Railroad at Niles; or, if he chose, he could take the triweekly, primitive train of the Milwaukee, Benton Harbor, and Columbus Railroad which chuffed through Berrien Springs to Buchanan. The mixed train could be flagged at any road crossing or farmhouse along the line.

THE MUCH-TRAVELED DEAN

The educator recounted how one mid-January day he took the triweekly train for Buchanan, where he planned to board the Michigan Central. However, the wreck of a freight train ahead blocked his train, and it was necessary for him to trudge through the deep snow with his grip. He was able to get a boy to help him, and he reached the village in time to catch an "accommodation train" to Niles, where he changed again, and arrived in Grand Rapids late that evening. Since trains were slow and irregular, connections had to be made at all hours of the night. Many diary entries, such as these, reveal strenuous nights of travel: "Took train for Chicago at 1:25 a.m.," "waited until 1:50 a.m. for No. 8," "left at 2 a.m. for Nashville."

Along with the weary journeys and the endless minutiae of operating the college, the president and the dean were continually harassed by the criticism of well-meaning souls who were certain they could operate the institution on a much better plan. In Battle Creek the feeling persisted that the college should never have been moved, while some ministers refused to encourage the young people of their congregations to attend Emmanuel Missionary College.

In May, 1903, the faculty were told by the president and dean that efforts were being made "to crush" the growing college. Naturally the continual waves of criticism eroded the morale of the families of the faculty. That spring Ida Magan became seriously ill. She recovered for a short time, but by July lapsed into a critical condition.

The deep personal tragedy struck Percy a devastating blow. He consulted with his medical friends, Drs. J. H. Kellogg and Paul Christman; but they held out no hope of any permanent restoration of Ida's health. Perhaps the best account of the situation was made in a lengthy letter by Magan to Ellen White. "Ida was taken ill quite suddenly on the night of Monday, June 1," he wrote. "The doctors pronounced the malady . . . acute, . . . brought on by over-anxiety and worry, and lack of nutrition. . . . She has always been a most devoted wife and mother, and, I believe, a sincerely good woman—quiet and unassuming. The death of her brother, about a year ago, just after he had graduated as a physician, was a great shock to her. This, together with my long sickness, and the recent reports which were circulated about me, I think, did the work.

"The great burden of her soul has been to bring her two little children up for God. It is hard for me to imagine how there could be a better mother than she has been to them. She was always a hard worker, doing her housework well. She made all her own clothes, and all the children's clothes. Every day she would read the Bible with them; tell them Bible stories, and pray with them, besides spending considerable time working with them in the garden in the summer, and teaching them in out-of-door work."

In September, after corresponding with Ida's mother, who lived in Santa Ana, California, Percy decided to take the boys to the west coast for the winter, while Mrs. Magan was left with those who could give her proper care. Sad farewells were said before the father and his sons took the train for Chicago. There, after Percy had replenished the boys' depleted wardrobe, the three began the long journey to southern California by way of San Francisco. The week's trip was an ordeal for the father, especially when Wellesley took sick with a fever of 102°. After only four days in California, Percy said good-bye to his boys. "I took the dear little children into my room, talked with them, prayed with them, and said farewell," he wrote in his diary. "Poor wee souls! My heart is so full for them; and dear Shaen sobbed so, as if his precious heart would break. It seems as if the last I have on earth is gone; I feel so lonely and sad."

On the way back to Michigan, he visited Mrs. White and her

son, Elder W. C. White, at Saint Helena. They counseled together concerning the expanding educational program of the church. The danger of molding Emmanuel Missionary College after the pattern of the average secular college was reemphasized by Mrs. White, as she and the educator drove through the autumn splendor of the Napa Valley and dined together at "Elmshaven." Such hours of counsel and the correspondence between Ellen White and the two educators were of inestimable value in holding the new college to basic concepts of Christian education. The admonition, though sometimes severe, was never refused by these men.

Instead of reaching Berrien Springs at the time he had planned, Percy was met in Chicago by Ed Sutherland, who told of serious matters brewing at the newly established General Conference headquarters in Washington, D.C.,* concerning the educational policies of the denomination. The dean went on to confer with the brethren in Washington and did not arrive home until the week school opened, when he found Ida "very frail."

As the fall term opened in 1903, the campus looked more pretentious. The Study Hall was completed, and seventy-five students attended the first service in the chapel. It had been a busy summer in construction work, picking and shipping grapes, canning vegetables and fruit for the college kitchen, and cutting wood for fuel.

SHADOWS OVER THE HOME

In November it was necessary for Percy to leave his wife in the hospital for extended treatment. In the ensuing months, when the devoted husband walked in deep shadows, he found one source of strength. "I must cling to God in living faith who doeth all things well," he said with confidence.

The testing fires of suffering had their effect upon the Irishman's character. He could say, "I know that these trials are sent to us not to bring bitterness out of our characters, but to bring all the fragrance that God can possibly bring into our lives, and I want the sorrows through which I am passing now to have this effect upon me." One Sabbath he spoke on the love of God to the college church; and in a chapel service the following Monday, he made a stirring appeal for consecration. Writing for the church paper, he declared, "The very

*The General Conference headquarters, which from the days of its inception in 1863 had been in Battle Creek, were in August, 1903, moved to Washington, the nation's capital. The Review and Herald office was also moved at that time.

experiences through which we have passed have only served to make its [the college's] walls and halls more dear."

With his wife in the hospital and his sons in California, Percy rented the lower floor of "Shamrock" to a faculty family. He boarded with the couple, who did their best to make the place homelike for him. To further relieve his financial burdens, the dean rented all the upstairs rooms "except the study and the little north bedroom."

It was a dreary winter; but to ward off any feeling of despair, Percy threw himself into greater activity on the campus, especially projects designed to strengthen the spiritual interests of the students.

During the winter of 1904, Ida contracted tuberculosis and grew progressively worse. A fever of 102° to 103° persisted each afternoon and evening, and because of her weakened condition Percy wrote, "We greatly fear that the poor child will not last long."

PROBLEMS AND PERSONAL LOSS

While personal anxiety pressed upon the dean, the problems of the college also increased. The 1904 Lake Union Conference session was to be held on the college campus in May, at which time the president and the dean planned to resign. They were convinced that they had made their contribution to Emmanuel Missionary College.

Since Mrs. White and her son, W. C., were planning to attend the union conference session, Percy cordially invited them and their secretarial help to stay at his home. "The brethren and sisters who are occupying my house have agreed with me to vacate this in behalf of you and your family," he wrote. "We are sorry that we have no better accommodations for you, but this is the best we can do. We will have a nice large bedroom on the south side of the house for you, and a room adjoining it for Sisters McEnterfer and Hare. . . . I am also planning that you can have my study which is a pleasant room on the south side of the house with a large veranda off it on the east side for your comfort and for meeting those with whom you may wish to visit and consult. . . .

"Brother and Sister Hill who occupy the downstairs of my house I am sure will be glad to do the cooking for your family, and we will have a phaeton and pony at your disposal all the time. If there is anything else which you think of that we can do for you please let us know and we will endeavor to be in readiness."

One May morning as Percy looked at the bed of wild strawberries, he remembered how Shaen "had found the plants in the woods, dug them up, hauled them in his little wagon to her [Ida], and asked if they could not plant them. Then they measured the ground together with his dear little brown 'hannies.' And now she lies dying. I cannot bear it."

Two weeks later, on the afternoon of May 19, Ida "peacefully passed away without a struggle. Dear, dear child," Percy wrote in his diary; "she is gone to her quiet rest, and all her sufferings ended." The funeral service was held in the Memorial Hall two days later, with Elders A. T. Jones, S. N. Haskell, G. I. Butler, A. G. Daniells, and William Covert, and Ellen White conducting the service.

On May 23 Mrs. White, in an address to the college church, praised the faithfulness of Ida Magan and rebuked those who had persistently criticized the educational program. The church leader said, "Sister Magan was so weighted down with sorrow. . . . This work of opposition and dissatisfaction [concerning the college] . . . has cost the life of a wife and mother."

The following day at the union conference session, Magan and Sutherland submitted their resignations as administrators of Emmanuel Missionary College. The board reelected the two men; but they felt that circumstances made the future success of their work at Berrien Springs precarious. In a letter to Ellen G. White, Magan had a few months earlier summed up the situation through which the educators had passed:

"During the last five or six years I feel that we have been passing through wars. We have had to encounter great opposition relative to leaving Battle Creek, relative to establishing the school at this place, and relative to making reforms in our educational system. True, our work has been experimental, but I know, as much as I know that I breathe, that God has been in it all, and that He will yet be glorified in this school, if we will walk humbly before Him and continue to advance in the light of Heaven's plans.

"But this constant turmoil and strife has had its effect on me in ways which I do not like, and I now feel an inexpressible desire in my soul to get rid of all the ill effects which it has had upon my character."

In all movements aimed at bringing about a new order of things there are varied viewpoints and differing attitudes even among trusted leaders. Some are apprehensive and hold back, some would drive too hard and too fast. Magan and Sutherland had made mistakes as they pioneered Christian education. Mrs. White had told the dean that he was sometimes afraid to call new members to join the faculty "for fear that they will counterwork your work," and she urged that "varied gifts" be brought to the college staff, and that he "give other men a chance" to get hold of the work.

After they resigned, the two educators were rebuked by Ellen White for their attitude at the union conference session. She said plainly: "There must be harmony between you and the men in responsible positions in the General Conference. You catch at straws in matters concerning Elder Daniells and Elder Prescott. Why?—Because they have not harmonized with you in all your plans, and have not given you the credit that you deserved. But when the Lord corrected errors, and spoke encouraging words concerning your efforts, why did you not praise Him, and show your gratitude by manifesting thankfulness and a forgiving spirit, and by showing an appreciation of the burdens borne by these fellow workers of God's appointment?"

Then, commenting on the fact that Sutherland and Magan were leaving the new school to begin work in another area, Ellen White declared that they did not leave "as men who have made a failure, but as men who have made a success." They "have acted in harmony with the light that God gave. They have worked hard under great difficulties. . . . They labored and toiled and sacrificed in their endeavor to carry out right lines of education. And God has been with them; He has approved of their efforts." In a second tribute, she said, "They have taught the students from the Bible, according to the light given from the *Testimonies*. The students that have been with them need not be ashamed of the education they have received."

A. W. Spalding later wrote of the establishment of the college: "It was a turning point in the educational history of Seventh-day Adventists. The vision and the courage and the resourcefulness which were demanded for this enterprise, breaking the bonds of custom and inertia, starting out on exploratory paths of education, breaking trail for adventurous and purposeful teaching, were worthy of all emulation by the rest of the church's schools. And to no little degree that course was taken."

The two men had long been interested in the advance of the church in the South. They had struggled to build a new Adventist college in Michigan, but now they were ready to place that work in other hands and accept another challenge in pioneering. Percy had a tempting offer from W. K. Kellogg, of Battle Creek, to join the expanding food factory. Recounting the cornflakes magnate's proposition in later years, Magan said, "He offered me a block of stock, $10,000 worth at par value. He wanted me to take charge of stock sales and offered me a commission on all I sold with a permanent place in the company when this work was done. That $10,000 of stock would be worth today somewhere in the neighborhood of $1,000,000 and, of course, trading on that I could have made it probably $3,000,000 or $4,000,000. The offer in a way was tempting. But I remember well spending the greater part of the night under a maple tree at old Berrien, then in the process of its own birth, and talking the whole matter over with the Master. And as the morning light broke I had decided it that in spite of all difficulties with brethren I must stick to this message and give whatever time and talent I had to the making of Adventists rather than to the making of cornflakes."

The ties with Berrien Springs were not broken until late in the summer of 1904, when Magan packed his household possessions and shipped them to Tennessee. He had come to the beautiful farm on the Saint Joseph River only three years before, hoping to fulfill his dream of founding a college according to the blueprint of Christian education. The hard-working, dedicated educator had seen the dream only partially fulfilled. He had arrived with his wife and sons; but the family circle was broken. Bowed by sorrow and disappointed at the turn of events, he was not dismayed. Dedicating his life to the message he loved, he would go forward in faith as a servant of God.

6

Another Pioneer Adventure

While still carrying the responsibilities of the new college, Percy Magan made a trip to the South. On June 1, 1904, he arrived in Nashville, where, during that month, he and Professor Sutherland surveyed the complex problems of establishing a self-supporting school. They were not unfamiliar with such pioneering, for they had already carved one college out of a Michigan farm. Fortunately, there were friends of the Adventist faith in the South who were ready to welcome and encourage the educators. Elder George I. Butler, president of the Southern Union Conference, was anxious to see the project succeed; and Percy's companion on the round-the-world tour, Elder S. N. Haskell, who was conducting evangelistic meetings in Nashville, was always a sponsor of Christian education.

The Southern States had caught the interest of Professors Sutherland and Magan as early as 1898, when Percy visited James Edson White, son of Ellen, who since 1894 had devoted his life to the education and evangelization of the colored people. The Irishman had cruised on the Cumberland River in Edson White's mission steamer, the *Morning Star*. Again in April, 1899, and June, 1901, the two educators went to Alabama and Tennessee to assist in planning small schools for colored children and to study existing institutions.

When Edson came to Battle Creek in 1899, Professor Magan helped him print his small journal, *The Gospel Herald*. In a letter to Ellen White, the dean told of how they at Battle Creek College were trying to do what they could to help Edson White in his work in the South. "We have taken a part of our old gymnasium," he wrote, "and have allowed him to fit up two nice little rooms out of a portion of it for offices and workrooms for himself, in which he can carry on correspondence with the churches, direct his work in the South, negotiate with the brethren for funds to carry on his work, et cetera. We have also been receiving a little money for the Southern field which we are using in connection with Edson and with his work."

The day after he arrived in Nashville, Professor Magan visited in

Edson's home, where he talked concerning the prospects for a school, with Mrs. White and her son, Willie, who were also spending a few weeks in the South. With their encouragement, the men were soon interviewing real-estate men and visiting farms that might be suitable for a school campus. Edson White proposed that the two educators take a trip up the Cumberland River in the *Morning Star* to view the country, and his mother agreed, saying, "It will be a good thing for you. You need the rest."

THE NELSON FARM IS CONSIDERED

On Thursday, June 9, the boat steamed up the river, but was forced to tie up at Edgefield Junction Landing, near Madison, for minor repairs. To while away the time, Edson's helper, W. O. Palmer, took Mrs. White to a nearby plantation, called the Nelson place (after former owners), a 414-acre farm which was being offered for sale at about $12,000. It was badly run-down, since much of the topsoil on the higher ground had been carried away by erosion, and the buildings and equipment were in need of repair.

The next day when Sutherland and Magan talked with Mrs. White, she told them she was impressed that the Nelson farm was the place for the school. "There is a farm here," she declared, "which the Lord wants you to have to start your school."

Amazed at the thought of purchasing such expensive property, the men protested. Since they had expected to go into the hill country and start a small school in one of the primitive areas, it was beyond their fondest hopes to think of opening a school on a broad campus some fifteen miles from Nashville! "It is out of the question!" they said.

The *Morning Star* continued up the river to Carthage, where the men spent two days looking at various farms. When the boat returned to Edgefield Junction, Mrs. White talked with the owners of the Nelson farm, an elderly couple named Ferguson. Then she persuaded Professors Sutherland and Magan to hold conferences with the Fergusons. On June 16 and 17, Magan endeavored to complete the purchase; but Mrs. Ferguson demanded more money. The problems Magan faced in attempting to close the sale are disclosed in his letter to Mrs. White: "We have been trying ever since we left the boat to close the deal for the Mat Allen farm, now owned by Mr. Ferguson. This is the farm you liked so well, and of which you said, 'We might search until we were gray-headed before we would find a better for our purpose.' We had the trade all closed once with Mr. Ferguson for $11,800. This included all farm implements, horses, cows, hogs, growing crops, et cetera. That night Professor Sutherland went north to get the money and that night I went over to meet Mr. Ferguson and have the contract signed by all parties concerned, but the devil had already begun to get his work in, and Mrs. Ferguson absolutely refused to sign the papers. . . . I spent all day Friday trying to fix the thing up with her. I finally got her to what I thought was a reasonable basis, although a higher price than her husband had made to us. She was so angry that she would not allow her husband in the room, and abused him in the most disgraceful manner. Three times she made me an offer, each one slightly different, and three times I accepted her offer, and three times she backed square out. Saturday night I went over and was there from a little after sundown until half past ten o'clock. I never went through more of a siege in my life. She now wants about $13,000 for the place. This, of course, is much more money than we had thought we could possibly pay, and yet on the whole, I think the place is better than any other place at that money."

As Magan had stated, his colleague, Professor Sutherland, had gone to Berrien Springs to get the financial backing of his aunt, Mrs. N. H. Druillard. Actually he had not been enthusiastic about the farm, especially when he compared it with the beautiful campus of Emmanuel Missionary College. When Sutherland had first surveyed the Nelson farm, he had said with tears in his eyes, "Percy, I can't do it. I can't undertake this. It's too big a job for us alone!"

The fighting Irish spirit welled up in Magan as he replied with courage, "Ed, we are in it—in it voluntarily. Mrs. White is with us. God is leading us. He will show us the way."

When Professor Sutherland described the plantation to his aunt, who had considerable money, she shook her head. It was risky and foolish, in her opinion, and she refused to promise a dollar for the purchase of the property. But when her nephew was about to return to Nashville, Aunt Nell weakened enough to say, "I'll go with you down there and look this thing over."

When Mrs. Druillard and Professor Sutherland arrived in Nashville, they went to the farm with Professor Magan. He records that "she liked it, and Ed likes it better." On this day, June 22, they drew up the agreement for the purchase at the price of $12,723, with a $5,000 payment to be made within ten days. The next day, with the financial aid of Aunt Nell, the two educators were able to get "everything signed." Thus Mrs. Druillard joined as a founder of the school, and she continued to support it and other church projects until she died at the age of ninety-four.

Although a site had been purchased, the two educators were not overly enthusiastic with the prospects for a school. Professor Sutherland said in later years, "If you had taken my heart on that day and turned it inside out, and scraped it with a surgeon's curette, and put it under the microscope, you could not have found the faintest premonition of what this place was to be."

A BUSY SUMMER

On the last day of June, Percy left Nashville for Chicago and Berrien Springs. About the time he arrived on the campus of Emmanuel Missionary College, an epidemic of smallpox struck, and he immediately arranged for the vaccination of all persons who had been exposed. There were numerous business matters for him to care for at Berrien Springs, Battle Creek, and Washington, D.C. While arranging for the incorporation of the Madison school, he counseled with Mrs. White and Elder Daniells. According to Percy's statements in his diary, the plans for the self-supporting school were not warmly received at the General Conference headquarters. Some of the leaders were fearful of the outcome of such a plan; others criticized the large amount of land that had been purchased; while still others could see no wisdom in a work-and-study program.

The issues were not clear in the minds of some of the leading men, and this formed a basis for apprehension. Magan and Sutherland had been linked with the reform in the educational program at Battle Creek and Berrien Springs which had substituted practical courses for many of the classical studies. Students at Battle Creek College and Emmanuel Missionary College were led into various industries with a program of work and study. At Berrien Springs, this culminated in a plan by which all faculty members went into the shops and the fields for a half of each day, to work with the students. Even in the face of the spirit of prophecy counsels which called for a work-study curriculum, some of the diehards entertained serious questions about such a program.

While the spirit of prophecy counsels, based on an insight of the future development of the work which others did not have, called for a sizable property for a college campus and a closely-linked agricultural program, there were those who found it difficult to recognize that a college really needed several hundred acres for its agricultural pursuits.

There was also the new policy of an institution's attempting to be financially self-supporting. There was the question of ownership and control. Sutherland and Magan had seen the General Conference Association through the late 1890's loaded down with debt on educational and medical institutions as they had passed their ever-increasing financial obligations to the Association. These two men had served for years as the leading officers at Battle Creek College, burdened with a debt of $90,000—a staggering amount in days when ministers and teachers worked for $10 or $12 a week. As they began work at Berrien Springs, the educators were determined to make the institution self-supporting—to build and expand no faster than funds were in hand.

Now these same men, Sutherland and Magan, with their "revolutionary" ideas, were about to start a self-supporting institution in the South. Some of the more conservative men were apprehensive.

After traveling through the South on her journey to the General Conference session of 1901, a field then comprised of three local conferences and half a dozen statewide missions, Ellen White had prepared an appeal entitled "Needs of the Southern Field." She wrote:

"In the South there is much that could be done by lay members of the church. . . . Let Sabbath-keeping families move to the South and live out the truth before those who know it not. These families can be a help to one another. . . . Let them do Christian help work, feeding the hungry and clothing the naked. . . . In many places schools should be established, and those who are tender and sympathetic, who, like the Saviour, are touched by the sight of woe and suffering, should teach old and young."

Enumerated among the subjects which should be taught were "how to till the soil," "how to cultivate various crops," and "how to plant and care for orchards." In response to this appeal some families moved into the South and in a quiet way settled in communities where they could radiate a positive influence for Christianity.

By 1904, with the exception of Kentucky and Tennessee with their combined membership of a thousand, none of the Southern States had as many as 300 members. In the light of this, the appeal for self-supporting families to go into the South is better understood. This was a challenge to Magan and Sutherland, who saw in the situation an opportunity to contribute to the church by the establishment of a school in Tennessee. Here they would endeavor to carry out the principles which they had championed—they would conduct a school where self-sacrificing young people could be trained for the work in the South. The Southern Union Conference was in no position to develop such a training center. Nor was the General Conference—then limited in resources, struggling to be free from debt, and rapidly expanding in a worldwide program—in any position to give strong financial support to this enterprise. Here indeed was a unique opportunity for a school operating on a self-supporting basis, and Sutherland and Magan were ready to test their ideas and principles of education. Where would they get money for land and buildings? How would the work be controlled? What would its relation be to the conference?

Elder George I. Butler, a seasoned church leader and president of the newly organized Southern Union Conference, welcomed the idea of such a school in his territory. Elder S. N. Haskell, longtime friend and fellow world traveler of Percy Magan, was located temporarily in the South, and he gave the educators a hearty welcome. But some leaders farther away, zealous that there should be no breach in organizational lines, entertained doubts and fears.

One delicate problem of a self-supporting institution, independent of direct guidance of the conference, was the source from which funds might be secured, especially for the purchase of property and the construction of buildings. Naturally the leaders of the new school thought of their friends and former associates who lived in areas where money flowed more freely. Appeals made from the South would, of course, lead to responses from the North and West. And it was not easy at times for those carrying the responsibilities of local work to stand by and watch sizable amounts of money being sent to another field.

Ellen White was clear in her counsel. As she saw it, the whole land was to be evangelized. She made it clear that consecrated Seventh-day Adventists whose work in a needy cause merited trust and confidence, doing a work which needed to be done, should not be restrained from obtaining gifts for the institution. The problems have since been largely solved, first, by the development of a strong denominational work in the South, a development in which self-supporting laborers have had a large part. Second, by the plan whereby conferences of limited resources receive aid from conferences in more favorable financial circumstances. Thus funds passing through the General Conference treasury pass from field to field.

Mrs. White called for general support of the project: "Let us sustain Brethren Sutherland and Magan in their efforts to advance this important work. They gained a valuable experience in Berrien Springs, and the providence of God has led them to feel that they must labor in the Southern field. God helped them constantly in their efforts at Berrien Springs, as they steadily advanced, determined that obstacles should not stop the work. They are not leaving Berrien Springs because of dissension or strife. They are not fleeing from duty. They are leaving a place where a school has been established, to go to a new field, where the work may be much harder.They have only means enough to pay part of the price of the land. They should not be left to struggle along misunderstood and unaided, at the sacrifice of health."

Before settling down to the strenuous program of the new school, which was incorporated under the name of the Nashville Agricultural and Normal Institute, Percy longed to visit his home in Ireland. His mother was growing old, and he had not seen her since the death of his father.

Several weeks of much-needed rest and relaxation in his native land helped him gain new strength as he enjoyed the association with those he loved.

THE FOUNDERS OF THE INSTITUTE

Before the first of February, 1905, Professor Magan was at Madison, ready to join the other three founders of the institute: Miss M. Bessie DeGraw, Mrs. Druillard, and Professor Sutherland. The Magan diary records the names of four students enrolled at the institute; however, before the school year ended, the student body numbered fifteen.

On the first letterhead of the Nashville Agricultural and Normal Institute were several pertinent statements, no doubt selected by the dean, as to the aims and purposes of the institution: "It is the object in establishing this school to correlate the intellectual, the physical, and the spiritual in education. . . . A strong intellectual course will be offered, including Bible, history, philosophy, and the sciences, the motto being 'learn by doing.' . . . Students are given an opportunity to support themselves while gaining an education, with a view to making them self-supporting Christian laborers when out of school."

There might have been a lack of students, but there was no end to the work. The weather was bitterly cold, with a heavy snow on the ground. One thing was needed—firewood—and Percy joined the woodcutters. Afterward he and Professor Sutherland set up stoves.

The old Plantation House of the estate had been built of cedar logs at the beginning of the nineteenth century, and a hundred years later it had been covered with clapboards and a coat of paint. The parlor, with rude furniture and no carpet, was the school chapel. Soon Mrs. Sutherland and young son Joe joined the group, and they all ate together, with Miss Olive Shannon acting as cook. In later years Professor Magan said the principal items on the bill of fare that first winter were buttermilk, corn bread, and cornmeal mush.

There was no aristocracy at the school. The president helped Elmer Brink, who had charge of the farm duties, while the dean worked in the timber with the boys. There may have been some criticisms as to the way individuals spent their time, for Percy began making daily entries in his diary as to the exact number of hours he spent in committees, in dictating, in cutting timber, and in performing countless other duties. He described his day's work in a letter to a friend: "I have no stenographer now, and do my own typing. While my right hand has not exactly lost her cunning, I am not quite as efficient at the business as when I pushed the pencil for a living in the Foreign Mission Board office fifteen years ago.

"Besides, when a man gets up at four-thirty in the morning and works in the field with a team of mules till one o'clock, and then goes at it again till six-thirty p.m., and then conducts a study for an hour or an hour and a half; takes the responsibility of planning the work for the boys, he is doing a pretty good day's work. And when it is taken into account that this has had to be done on old, and rather worn-out land, with a goodly sprinkle of rocks and thornbushes, and by one who has not followed the farming business since he was eighteen years of age, I, at least, find that it has taxed my determination of purpose, and capacity to meet and overcome hard problems even more than heading a Relief of Schools campaign. . . . But the whole has been a great experience, and I feel more genuine iron determination, and grim strenuosity in my bones today to take hold of things which need to be done and to do them than I have ever felt in my life before."

Miss DeGraw acted as a secretary for the administrators, and once a week she drove to town in a mule cart to sell the butter that had been churned in the primitive creamery. Mrs. Druillard, treasurer, supervised the domestic duties of the institute. Percy Magan frequently drove to Nashville in the cart with a load of fresh produce and eggs, which he peddled from door to door. During the first year, class discussions centered around methods of making a farm pay (they weren't too sure they could!) how to bring livestock through the winter, and methods of soil cultivation and crop growth.

By the middle of March, 1905, the farm crew were planting trees for a future orchard—two hundred apple and "a lot of peach, pear, and plum" trees. It was a catastrophe when Rhoda, the mule, became lame. There may have been additional farm animals; but it was necessary to hire a wagon and team for $2 a day in order to haul lumber for new buildings.

Professor Magan seemed to know how to grapple with farm problems. There were loganberry roots to plant, 1,800 strawberry plants to set out, and melons, squash, and other vegetables to get started. He supervised the student crews, bought the seeds or plants, and directed the spreading of the fertilizer. It was a time of forced economy, when faculty and students alike joined in working long hours and in dreaming of brighter days ahead. If Professors Sutherland and Magan were not working on the farm or supervising the handful of students, they were traveling among the churches in money-raising campaigns.

A joint article prepared by the educators set forth the purpose of the project in these words: "It is the purpose of this new school to demonstrate to young men and women desirous of doing their Master's service that they can begin a work for Him without the aid of any special equipment, and with only the common buildings to be found on almost any farm. It is our prayer that this school may be a factor in developing self-reliant, self-supporting missionary work. Those who are founding it do so without the promise or assurance of specific support or a definite salary from any source." Whether the students would achieve the ends desired was still problematical; but it was certain that after the first year of strenuous labor, both physical and mental, the founders knew more about self-reliance, self-support, and the lack of a definite salary! But their sacrifice faded into the background when they envisioned an institution which would offer many a youth in the South a practical, Christian education.

AN IOWA SCHOOLTEACHER

A demure Iowa public-school teacher arrived in Battle Creek in the autumn of 1891. This twenty-one-year-old girl, named Lillian

Eshleman, had been urged by her elder sister Emma, the wife of Joseph Rosseau, to attend Battle Creek College. The Rosseaus were spending a year at the college before they sailed for Australia to help advance the church, and Emma was anxious to see her younger sister in the Adventist school.

Lillian was born in Dixon, Illinois, March 25, 1870, the tenth child in a family of eleven children. The Eshleman family settled on an Iowa farm; but since the father believed his sons and daughters should receive an education, they moved into the town of Cherokee when Lillian was twelve. The precocious girl was graduated from high school, took all the teacher-training courses available, and taught public school for three years.

When Lillian went to Battle Creek, she was not a Seventh-day Adventist. Her parents were Lutherans, but she had attended the Presbyterian church. The girl was anxious to complete the normal course, with emphasis upon classes in science and literature. She was disappointed when she found that the Adventist college specialized in Greek, Latin, mathematics, and logic. However, she accompanied her sister to the professor of history and Bible, hoping to find a solution to her problem. Lillian, in later years, described her first impression of Professor Magan: "I met a young man of twenty-three," she said, "slender, dignified, and immaculately groomed, with a thick, well-trimmed pompadour haircut, and black broadcloth suit. He had a serious mein; and when I told him my troubles, he said, "I'm sorry, but I teach only history and Bible.' "

The charming young lady informed the professor that she had taken basic history courses and did not look with enthusiasm on additional subjects which merely reviewed military maneuvers and required the memorizing of the dates of battles. "I would like to know something of the meaning of history," insisted Lillian.

"Well," replied the young professor, weakening before the feminine charmer, "that comes in the third year; but if you do not intend to take the regular course I might take you in that class."

The new student asked if she might also enroll in a Bible class. The teacher said, "Your schedule is full, but you may come to my classes in Bible if you can arrange your schedule." Lillian arranged her program and attended the class.

A few weeks before the college year closed, she was converted while in quiet study in her room. Lillian knelt in prayer, earnestly saying, "Lord, I believe. Help Thou my unbelief." Many of the promises of the New Testament passed through her mind, and these answered the nagging questions that had plagued her. She found peace through the way of eternal life, and was baptized by Elder Alonzo T. Jones.

Returning home in the spring, she decided to teach school again, since she lacked the finances for another year of college. On the weekends, Lillian studied the Bible with her mother, presenting the doctrines in a systematic way, and in due time the mother also became a loyal Seventh-day Adventist.

IN THE NURSING PROFESSION

After another year of study at Battle Creek College, Lillian entered the nurses' training course at the sanitarium in July, 1894. Her college credits made it possible for her to take the special two-year course. Before the training was completed, however, she was called to be the Minnesota Conference nurse. This was a new position in conferences, and Dr. Kellogg was anxious for a capable young woman to make a success of the job. A Scandinavian classmate, Maren Johansen, also accepted the call, and the two young women worked during the winter of 1895 and through the next spring and summer until after camp meeting, conducting cooking schools, teaching classes in healthful living, first aid, and the giving of simple treatments. They featured hydrotherapy treatments by showing the way fomentations could be given in the home with a washboiler and how leg baths could be taken in garbage cans! Lillian modeled the healthful dress, which included no corset, no tight bands, no sweeping skirts, and no high heels. The two young women certainly earned the $5 a week which the conference paid them.

Since she had not completed the course in nursing, Lillian was anxious to return to Battle Creek. She wrote Dr. Kellogg, "I've told everything I know so many times I must learn something more." The doctor enthusiastically replied, "Come back and take the medical course."

Going forward by faith, but with little money, Lillian returned to Battle Creek to enter the freshman class in medicine in 1896. She worked in the Sanitarium office and in Dr. Kellogg's medical library to earn money for all her expenses. In addition to the classes, her office duties, and the endless hours of study, Lillian said, "I worked a couple of hours each day [for Dr. Kellogg], and on Saturday nights from sundown to midnight, when he had his secretary come to his home where he dictated while I passed marked material to him." In 1900 she was graduated and began practicing as a resident physician at the sanitarium at a salary of $30 a month.

THE DOCTOR SAID "YES"

When the Battle Creek Sanitarium was rebuilt in 1902, after the fire, Dr. Eshleman was one of the resident physicians for the 500 patients. In the months after the establishment of the Madison school, Professor Magan, going frequently to Battle Creek on business, found opportunity to renew his acquaintance with his former student. The friendship blossomed into a romance, and the charmingly feminine doctor and the intrepid educator were engaged. The entry in Percy's diary for September 30, 1904, read: "Went for a walk with L. [Lillian], who gave final promise."

It must have required a great deal of courage on the part of Percy to ask a successful physician, connected with the famous Battle Creek Sanitarium, to give up a promising professional career to move to the South, where the hazardous program of a self-supporting school was being tested. But Dr. Lillian, dedicated to the service of God and her fellowmen, was ready to begin a life of adventure with the companion she loved. However, because of the uncertainty of the Madison project, then only in its beginning, the couple decided it would be wise to wait a year before their marriage.

At six o'clock on the hot summer evening of August 23, 1905, Percy and Lillian were married at her home in Cherokee, Iowa. Their honeymoon of a little over a week included a buggy ride in the country, visits with the bride's relatives, three days of shopping and sight-seeing in Chicago, and a preaching appointment for the bridegroom in the Cherokee Presbyterian church. On September 4 the newlyweds arrived in Nashville, where Ed Sutherland welcomed them at the railroad station with the milk cart drawn by a mule!

Soon after the Magans arrived at Madison, the Sutherlands, Mrs. Druillard, and Miss DeGraw moved out of Plantation House to three new cottages. It was the lot of the newlyweds, however, to occupy one of the three upstairs bedrooms in the antique dwelling. Dr. Lillian well remembered that there was no running water, no bathroom, no carpet, no clothes closets; there were kerosene lamps for light and a small wood-burning stove for heat. The room had been used by former owners as a place to cure and dry tobacco. One of the first tasks the young bride took upon herself was to scrub the stained poplar floor with buckets of water carried from the well. The more she scrubbed, the more pungent the odor that rose from the tobacco-soaked wood. When Percy came in from the farm, he asked, "What have you been doing to stir up such an aroma?" He was joined by Mrs. Druillard, who warned Dr. Lillian to stop her scrubbing before the moisture seeped through the ceiling and stained the living room, which was the school's largest classroom!

Within a short time the bride was hard at work in routine duties; but she took time to write and pass the examinations of the Tennessee State Medical Board. Soon she was being called by Dr. Hayward of the Nashville Sanitarium to assist in surgery and as a consultant on numerous cases.

Determined to move out of their one-room apartment as soon as possible, the Magans set to work in late September building a cottage in a grove of trees. Carpenters did the heavy construction, but Dr. Lillian and her husband laid the floors, lathed the rooms (except the ceilings), and did the sandpapering, painting, and finishing. Percy was anxious to bring his sons, Wellesley and Shaen, from California as soon as a suitable home was prepared, and Dr. Lillian was equally anxious to mother the boys.

MOVING INTO A NEW HOME

The seventeenth of January, 1906, was a memorable day for the Magans. On that morning they moved from the Plantation House into their new home, which Percy named "Unavarra," after an estate in Ireland. The house had four rooms on the ground floor and three semi-attic rooms. The couple were diplomatic in not calling it a "two-story house," for on the campus such a dwelling was "taboo in those days," as it set families in a higher social status. However, Dr. Lillian had her medical office in one of the upstairs rooms, and the other two were prepared for the boys when they came from the west coast.

The founders had now passed the worst pioneering experiences. Their first tables had been planks laid on sawhorses, their dressers were rejuvenated dry-goods boxes, and chairs or stools were scarcely two of a kind. In the first months, when there had been few accommodations for students, the weather-beaten barn, nicknamed "Probation House," had been the temporary dormitory for newcomers.

In describing the founders—Professors Sutherland and Magan, Mrs. Druillard, and Miss DeGraw—Dr. Lillian said, "They possessed distinct and positive personalities, but they were united in one purpose.

Their association together in Berrien Springs had taught them to value each other's capabilities and to overlook the other's idiosyncracies." (Percy often said the word meant, "I do sin so crazy.")

Here, then, was an unusual and talented group of men and women, individual in their thinking, but banded together in a self-sacrificing enterprise. Certainly they had no precedent in Seventh-day Adventist ranks for such a self supporting educational institution.

Dr. Lillian joined her husband in every phase of the work of the growing school. She was a teacher, homemaker, school physician, and a busy doctor going to the sanitarium or attending medical meetings to keep up with the expanding knowledge in her profession. Yet in all her versatile activities she never overshadowed her husband; she determined that the Magan family would be known because of Percy's work, not hers.

7

Building in Spite of Difficulty

No one but the founders of the Nashville Agricultural and Normal Institute will ever know the financial stringency they faced during the pioneer days of the institution. Many times it seemed that they could not possibly make the payments on the farm. In an article in the *Review and Herald,* Miss DeGraw explained some of the difficulties. "When our company bought the farm," she wrote, "we thought we knew where we would get the money to pay for it. We were to borrow a part, and the rest was due the different members from our various institutions [to whom the members had lent money]. We felt sure that the payment of the land was practically provided for. We made the first payment with our borrowed money. We had three other installments to make, then an old mortgage to deal with. As the time of the payments drew near, we found that our institutions could not let us have the money without embarrassment. We could not crowd these branches, for we had the same interest in their prosperity that we had in this. Often the way looked dark, and it seemed that there was nothing to do but sell part of the farm."

Friends close to the founders, such as Elder Haskell and Mrs. White, counseled against selling any part of the plantation to meet the payments. In the critical days, when only faith was strong, persons devoted to Christian education lent money without interest or at a low rate, and the obligations were paid on time.

In February, 1906, a report on the progress of the school was given to Mrs. White by Professor Magan. He said, "We have been waiting long and praying earnestly that the Lord would open up the way in some way for us to have a sanitarium out here. But it has taken all the strength we have had, and all the means we could rake and scrape together to get things going in the school. . . .

"We have a splendid class of students and they are gaining a good experience. Two of our number have recently gone to Cuba. They will study the language, and work with their hands and canvass till they can see some way open to do more. . . . We are endeavoring to train workers in the simple things of the third angel's message. We teach them the Bible, physiology and hygiene, the English language, church history, the keeping of accounts, and how to give simple treatments. We are planning that no girl shall leave our school who is not a good cook, and able to make her own clothes, and do simple nursing for the relief of the sick. We endeavor to have each one have an experience in canvassing for our books. To some these things do not look like an education at all. They think our school is cheap, and that we should pay more attention to the things of the world taught in books, to Latin and Greek and the like. . . . .

"Lately we have been following a new plan which our life in the country makes feasible: We can buy three cows for $100, and the butter which we get from three cows will support a boy in school for a year. We own the cows, but our students do the work of milking, butter making, and caring for them. In this way we are able to support them in school without any loss to ourselves, and the cows and their increase form a perpetual endowment for the benefit of the students in the school. . . .

"God is teaching us many lessons of economy. We have exceedingly little to do with, but that is all the better, as it makes us all, both teachers and students, careful of every little that we do have. Besides, it will give our students a solid training in poverty and hardness, hardship and self-denial which will be invaluable to them when they go out into the work. I long to see noble men and women go forth from our schools, inured to hardship and toil, and afraid to go nowhere on earth where they may be called in their Master's service."

ON WHEELS RECRUITING AND RAISING FUNDS

The dean made frequent trips of from four to ten weeks' duration, interesting young people in education for service in the South, and visiting churches and individuals who might give money to the institute. In some states he was barred by conference committee action from soliciting. He usually spent the summer months at camp meetings, while in the winter he toured the Dakotas and Canada, a grueling itinerary that tested his physical endurance. At camp-meeting time he was drawn into the regular program, often speaking several times in a day. Two and three sermons a day, long drives by horse and sled through storms, nights of travel on rickety trains—no wonder Percy fought colds, influenza, and more serious illness!

Of one of his trips, Professor Magan wrote: "I do not know that I ever had in all my life more blessed experience preaching the gospel of Jesus Christ than this summer. . . . I asked for but very little money for our work and got very little, but made a great many friends, and got some fine people to come south."

During the autumn of the same year he was again in South Dakota: "I got pretty well run down up in South Dakota, as it has been the most severe winter they have had in many years, and many times I had to make drives in the bitter cold, on top of three or four feet of snow from fifteen to forty miles at a time. I have been trying to get my nerves back since I returned, and seeing it is not the season for agriculture, have betaken myself to hammer and saw."

The educator attempted to quiet the fears of any persons who thought he might be using "high-pressure methods" to raise funds for the school. "I note your hope that my moderation in the matter of pulling for gifts for the Madison school will work out for the benefit of the school later on," he declared. "We can only trust the Lord over that, but one thing I know: that David was right when he said, 'I will behave myself wisely.' I did not receive as much as one cent for the Madison school, or any of its founders, teachers, or promoters at any camp meeting this summer. I believe that by pursuing a policy of getting along with just as little means as possible until certain principles are more clearly seen, understood, and appreciated of the greatness of God's work and His manifold ways of working, that the unity of this cause will be better accomplished by pursuing this policy than by in any sense asserting our rights. I am far more anxious that right principles be recognized by men at the head of the work than that we should have all the money we need. I know I could have gotten large sums of money this summer; but I have thought very much on one expression in one of those testimonies which Mother [Ellen White] gave me while in California, namely: 'Our great need is unity; we have not one soul that can be spared. The Lord calls upon us to unify in harmony with Bible truth. This should be repeated over and over in the family and in the church.' "

There was a feeling of accomplishment—the reward for days and weeks of effort—effort which resulted eventually in cash, pledges, and deeds to property being directed to Madison. Students and teachers were cheered by Professor Magan's reports of successful fund-raising experiences. And the school plant was growing, for in 1908 eight cottages were built to house thirty-six students, and buildings were erected for a bathroom and laundry, a bakery and a dairy.

Four cottages had also been completed by faculty members for their families.

In spite of his nerve-racking program, Percy Magan did not slight his spiritual development. His New Year's resolution for 1907 was a pledge to devote more time to the study of the Scriptures. He wrote in his diary: "Began a systematic reading of the Bible. Planned to read ten chapters per day. There are 889 chapters in the Old Testament and 260 in the New. Total 1,149. This means the completion of the reading of the Bible in about four months."

His sermon topics continued to be fresh and original; as a student of history, he was alert to current events. He spoke many times on the Eastern question, Turkey, and other topics of current interest as they related to Bible prophecy. In September, 1908, he was chosen to serve as associate editor of the journal, *The Watchman,* published weekly in Nashville by the Southern Publishing Association. A perusal of this published material reveals the author's wide reading and diligent scholarship.

On April 7, 1907, the Magans left the campus "to get the bairnies," who were still at their grandmother Bauer's home in California. Dr. Lillian had worked at the Hinsdale Sanitarium for a time to earn enough extra money to make the trip with her husband. Before the couple left, however, it was imperative for them to help pick the site of the Rural Sanitarium, which was to be built on the campus. Several years earlier Mrs. White had encouraged the founding of such a medical institution when she wrote: "Whenever it is possible to have a school and a sanitarium near enough together for helpful cooperation between the two institutions, and yet separated sufficiently to prevent one from interfering with the work of the other, let them be located so as to carry on their work in conjunction."

There was no end to the manual work for every member of the family. Indeed, when Percy returned from one of his trips, he noted that he brought home rubber boots for his wife!

Spring and summer of 1907 were disappointing seasons for the farmers of Tennessee. At the school farm the wet, cold spring killed the alfalfa and forced the replanting of the corn. Then the intense heat and drought of summer seared the pastures and dried up the sorghum crop so that there was only a third the normal yield. "This, of course, makes the second hard year in succession for us from the standpoint of the farm," said Professor Magan. "We are not having nearly as much butter as we ought to have to sell; this has cut down our income. Our garden was practically a failure, but we are no different from the people all around us. The terrible drought simply killed peas, beans, and practically all the other garden vegetables. Potatoes have done nothing on account of the drought and are now $1.50 a bushel in Nashville. . . . We have had considerable difficulty in pumping water for our stock. . . .

"Besides this, the terrifically hot weather has had its effect upon both teachers and students. We have had more sickness this year than any year since we have been here. . . .

"You will be interested to know that I am getting to be quite an expert butter maker. Aunt Nell has been initiating me in all the arts and mysteries and difficult sciences of lacteal germs, ripening, molding, et cetera. Our butter is winning us a good deal of praise in Nashville, and we are in hopes that in another year we will be sufficiently advertised to command better prices."

Of his more scholarly duties, the dean made these observations: "I am teaching a Bible class every day, supplying an article every week to the *Watchman,* . . . and doing what I can in the way of personal work with the students, a work which I love, and which I feel is much neglected in most of our schools, our own not exempted." As if all his duties on the campus were not enough, the educator gave a series of Sunday-evening lectures in Nashville on the Eastern question and Bible prophecies, with gratifying attendance.

Extra burdens also fell on the dean's shoulders when in the fall his colleague left the campus because of illness. In October, 1907, Magan reported: "Professor Sutherland is still away and very, very poorly. He is letting business matters as far as we are concerned entirely alone."

PROBLEMS FACING THE SELF-SUPPORTING WORK

As alluded to in another chapter, the relation of the denomination to the self-supporting schools of the South had been a subject of concern among church leaders from the inception of the program. Mrs. White wrote, "We greatly desire the prosperity of the work in the South." And concerning the Madison school, she declared, "I have every confidence that it was our duty to purchase this land. Let us not worry. The necessary means will be provided."

At the Southern Union Conference session held in Nashville in January, 1908, Elders Daniells and Griggs and other church leaders reviewed the development of the institute, studied its charter, and gave the project a clean bill of health. The conference gave a vote of confidence to the school and pledged cooperation, while the president of the General Conference called for unity of spirit and assured the founders that the institute would continue untrammeled. The conference voted to appropriate $19,500 to the Madison school, an action which greatly encouraged the faculty and students.

EVEN PROBLEMS HAVE A TOUCH OF HUMOR

On the lighter side of the picture, one finds humor in some of the campus discipline. It was necessary to hold faculty meetings to discuss an evening fudge party given by secretaries in their office for some young masculine admirers. There was the talk which Professor Magan had with one young woman who had allowed a young man to come to her room in order that she might curl his hair! The girl was almost expelled over this indiscretion, but the administration decided to give her "another opportunity" to prove her citizenship in the school.

An epidemic of smallpox struck the student body during the winter of 1908, brought unwittingly to the campus by two students—a young man and his sister—who had arrived from South Dakota. Dr. Lillian examined the boy and his sister and another girl who had broken out with confluent smallpox. Mother D went with the doctor to the cottage where the sick were isolated; but when the business manager found that these were cases of genuine smallpox, she left the cottage hurriedly and did not reappear until many days later, when all the sickness had disappeared!

Dr. Lillian summoned the county health officer, who immediately quarantined the student body. This was the first contact the school had made with Nashville physicians, and the health officer was very cooperative. Dr. Lillian, with the help of two nurses, brought eight cases of the dread disease through without a casualty.

In spite of the seriousness of the smallpox, the experience had positive results in forging a link with medical authorities of the area, a relationship that was of great value in later days. Indeed, the students, teachers, and administrators of the school were becoming more conscious of the need to combine medical work with education. Mrs. White had envisioned a small sanitarium on the Madison campus, where "the educational work at the school and the sanitarium can go forward hand in hand." By 1909, the modest sanitarium was "practically full of patients, among others the dean of the dental department of Vanderbilt University." Dr. Lillian was busy with a full-time practice, although her health was not the best.

When Percy made the trip to California in 1907, he had visited Loma Linda, where he saw the beginnings of the denomination's medical work in the West. At that time he confided to Elder W. C. White: "I feel a deep interest in the work at Loma Linda; and I wish I could be there, but that is out of the question." However, the realization of the need to develop medical facilities at Madison increased the desire of Magan and Sutherland to be physicians who could serve the sick and instruct students.

8

Things Medical

From its inception the institute at Madison aimed to give students practical courses in healthful living. The first class in nursing consisted of five girls who received instruction from Mother D in a primitive treatment room in the old Plantation House. Hydrotherapy, massage, bed making, handling of patients, and the principles of a healthful diet were covered in the course. Early in the history of the Madison school, Ellen White had urged the beginning of sanitarium work.

The first sanitarium on the campus grew out of the request of a Nashville businessman for a place to rest and receive simple treatments amid rural surroundings. The sanitarium cottage soon became too small, and in 1908 additional cottages were erected. The plan of the sanitarium was simple—the buildings were on one floor with wings extending from the central corridor to form patios and sheltered areas. Church officials from the Southern Union Conference and from the General Conference were present at the dedicatory ceremonies on October 18, 1908.

Dr. Lillian Magan was appointed director of the medical institution, and her husband records how a committee held a two-day session before it could decide to allow her the munificent salary of $13 a month, the same as the founders! The doctor was also guaranteed 10 percent of the gross medical fees received, provided the amount did not exceed $80 a month. (Dr. Lillian remembered definitely that her salary never reached that figure!)

The expanding medical program soon required additional personnel, and Dr. Newton Evans, a Seventh-day Adventist physician teaching pathology in the University of Tennessee Medical School, at Nashville, was appointed superintendent of the sanitarium.

Shortly after the dedication ceremonies for new sanitarium buildings, Professor Magan left on an extended Midwest tour to campaign for $9,500, the sum necessary to complete the basic school plant. Only a few weeks before he left the campus, he made this unusual entry in his diary: "Have been home a year with exception of trip to Washington, D.C., and Stuart, Iowa." He mentioned an interesting sidelight on this trip, which he made in the fall of 1908—his first ride in an automobile. He took this ride while he was visiting Dr. C. P. Farnsworth at Chamberlain, South Dakota. While the two men were chugging along the road to inspect an Indian school, the car broke down. Magan described in one word how they solved the transportation problem: "Walked."

During those years Professor Magan developed a friendship with Elder J. W. Christian, president of the South Dakota Conference, and the bond grew as the educator and the conference president visited churches and families in South Dakota. "I had a good time in the Northern Union, as I always do," wrote the Irishman. "I promised to give them three weeks. Elder John Christian and I worked together, and had a very good time. The Lord blessed us and moved upon the hearts of the people to give. At the end of the three weeks we had $24,600. Of course, the people in South Dakota are not rich as they are in California, but they gave what they had most willingly. There were two $1,000 gifts, two $800, two $700, and several $600." Elder Christian was ever a promoter of the Madison school program, and he assisted the founders in every way possible. In 1907 the Christians named their newborn son Percy, after their Irish friend.

AN EXPANDING MEDICAL PROGRAM

Far to the west, at Loma Linda, California, a sanitarium had been purchased in May, 1905, and the next year arrangements were made to open a school to train "workers in connection with the sanitarium." Since the sanitarium on the Madison campus had developed a similar interest in medical evangelism, Professors Sutherland and Magan wondered if they might make a greater contribution to the church if they took the medical course. Dr. Newton Evans, living with his family on the Madison campus while he was director of the Madison Sanitarium and professor at the University of Tennessee Medical School, urged his two friends to study medicine.

However, the problems facing the educators seemed almost insurmountable. Age was not in their favor, for in 1910 Sutherland was forty-six and Magan was forty-two. Professor Magan sought counsel from Elder W. C. White, and Mrs. Druillard talked about the plan with Ellen White. The educator's view of the important decision is revealed in his correspondence. "The whole matter has been one of great perplexity to me and I have prayed over it much," he wrote. "We both feel that it is a great undertaking at our age and especially in view of our heavy responsibilities in the school. Our situation is a difficult one. As our work in the hills grows we realize more and more the great need of equipping our hill school teachers as medical evangelists. . . .

"These conditions have in the past led us to endeavor to connect a man doctor with us; but in this we have not been successful. This class of worker does not seem willing to sacrifice the way we feel we have to—they make demands on us that we cannot meet. My wife, of course, does all she can, but she is not strong, and cannot, of course, lead out like a man.

"The question may arise in your mind as to why both of us should take upon us the burden of preparing for this line of work. We have felt that though hard for the present it would be easier on us in the long run than if only one of us took it. We will both be able to attend to considerable work in the school while studying."

When Elder White wrote an encouraging report to Magan's proposal, he in turn replied: "I cannot tell you what an encouragement your letter was to both Professor Sutherland and myself. We have prayed a great deal over the matter of the medical work, and earnestly prayed that the Lord would lead us to do just the right thing. I have always had a kind of horror of a man who has been engaged in the ministry for years taking up the medical work or any other line of work, as he may have less interest in the ministerial work and not amount to very much in the medical work. We feel, however, that God has a special mission for us in the medical work. I do not intend to give up the ministry. I intend to continue my study and research. But as you say, the time has come for a great medical evangelical movement, and I do not see how this is going to be unless some of those who have had experience in the evangelical work take up the medical work. . . .

"We did not enter the Vanderbilt as we had intended but have entered the medical department of the University of Tennessee, where Dr. Evans is teaching. This is just as good a school, and there are some advantages to us. We did not get any special favors. We did not ask for them, as we did not think it best. We told the dean just why we wanted to take the course. . . . The sanitarium here has made us known more or less, which is an advantage to us. . . .

"You asked about the tuition at the school. The tuition is $130 a year. It takes about $60 a year for books, and the carfare is about $8 a month, but Dr. Evans is going to get an auto and will carry

Sutherland and myself at a much lower rate. The financial drain on us will be heavy, and neither Sutherland nor myself can see our way through or anything like through. We get together enough to pay only one half of the tuition for the first year, and we know that the Lord will open up the way when we need more."

The operation and financing of the Madison school continued to demand wise leadership, and it was decided that the two feminine founders, Mrs. Druillard and Miss DeGraw, with Dr. Lillian and the school's department heads, would keep the institution moving ahead. Since the university was only nine miles from Madison, the men would commute part of the time between their homes and their classes.

The teachers were cooperative, and some of them shifted their Saturday classwork to other days to accommodate the two Adventists. Some of the association with students was not conducive to the highest ideals. "I think I realize more than ever before the necessity of Sister White's warning our young people against going to these medical schools," Magan declared. "They are certainly bad places, although there are many good people connected with them. There is such smoking, chewing, swearing, coarse and obscene language. Nevertheless the work has opened up to me truths which I have read in the Bible . . . in a way that is little short of marvelous. I pray to God that these experiences may only substantiate the truths in the Bible. . . . We have not taken up this work because we wanted something easier, or because we are tired of the work we are now doing, but only that we might be able to do that work better."

When he began the second year of medicine in the fall of 1911, he purchased a Pierce motorcycle on which he often commuted. He wanted to be at home as much as possible, for Dr. Lillian was expecting in January. The motorcycle trips were not all pleasant, however, even when both medical students had machines, for the engines sometimes balked. Muddy roads or the rough crushed-rock surfacing often made the going treacherous.

THE ARRIVAL OF VAL

On January 19, 1912, Percy attended medical school classes as usual; but at noon he received a telephone call urging him to hurry home. The diary tells the story: "Lillian brave as a lion. Did fine and baby boy, six and a half pounds [delivered] at 5:26 p.m." Val O'Connor, the "wee stranger," kept his father home the next forenoon; but that evening the medical student was back in the laboratory at Nashville. By this time the two men had rented a room in the city, where they stayed during the week, studying long hours without interruption.

In April, the week of the sinking of the *Titanic,* Percy came home from classes at Nashville with a "cold on his chest." Some days before, he had plowed his way through a blustery snowstorm on his motorcycle and as the result was severely chilled. The chest cold proved to be more serious than he thought, and when Dr. Lillian called in their good friend Dr. Evender Sanders for consultation, he pronounced it bronchial pneumonia with pleurisy near the diaphragm. Because baby Val was also sick at this time, Dr. Lillian arranged for a nurse for each patient, and she endeavored to divide her time between them.

A sincere woman in the community visited Professor Magan while he was recovering and confided all her troubles to him, which almost caused a relapse. As she was leaving she said to Dr. Lillian, "You will take good care of him, won't you? We surely need him." Somehow the tired and patient wife felt that "we" should be baby Val and herself!

When the University of Tennessee moved to Memphis in 1912, the two educators arranged to transfer their junior year of study to Vanderbilt University School of Medicine, making it possible for them to remain in Nashville. These were nine hectic months, for in addition to lectures, clinical work, and study, the educators faced a rising tide of misapprehension concerning the self-supporting school program. As Magan expressed it, some of the leaders in the church feared "a kingdom within a kingdom." But the two educators had faced many a difficulty, and they pushed ahead undaunted.

The autumn of 1913 found Magan and Sutherland at Memphis, where they completed their senior year with their original class. They lived in the Washington Street home of Kate Lawler, who was evidently an eccentric Irishwoman. Because of the heavy schedule, they were unable to be on the Madison campus except for a few weekends and the Christmas vacation. However, the enrollment of the institution continued to climb, and Miss DeGraw could report: "The Madison school is working quietly, steadily, for the preparation of practical missionaries."

By this time the annual convention of self-supporting workers was bringing together some 250 delegates, mostly from local mountain schools where Madison students were pioneering Christian education. There were workers, however, from as far away as Honduras.

A librarian from Nashville, enthusiastic about practical education, had been a patient at the sanitarium and an observer of the school. When she married Dr. P. P. Claxton, United States Commissioner of Education, she suggested that part of their honeymoon be spent on the Madison campus where her husband could study the project. Later Dr. Claxton wrote of the institute: "There *are* new things, and here is one: a school that is self-supporting; a school that receives no aid from public or invested funds, and asks none; a school that young men and women may enter without money, finish standard courses of study under well prepared teachers, gain practical experience for life and for making a living, and leave unhampered by debt; a school that has succeeded in making all instruction definite, attractive, inspiring, and practical; a school that has succeeded in dignifying labor and making it highly profitable both educationally and financially. . . . Here students, teachers, and directors, working together, constitute a self-supporting, democratic, educational community, the like of which I do not know—a fulfillment of the hopes and dreams of educators and philanthropists. I have seen many schools of all grades in many countries, but none more interesting than this. Nowhere else have I seen so much accomplished with so little money."

The sanitarium also was gaining prestige. Magan reported in August, 1914: "Governor Ben Hooper of the State of Tennessee has been with us several times during the last year. Mr. Jordan Stokes, one of the most noted lawyers in all the South, has had his wife and other members of his family here for weeks."

A DOCTOR OF MEDICINE

On June 6, 1914, the two Madison administrators celebrated their graduation from medical school, and since this was an era before internships were required, Dr. Magan immediately entered practice. Dr. Lillian declared that he was a brilliant diagnostician, who would have been a skilled internist because of his retentive memory and burning desire to gather all pertinent facts concerning the patient and the cause of his illness. The doctor gained the respect of the physicians at the sanitarium and in Nashville because of his careful, accurate diagnoses.

During these years, Shaen, three years younger than Wellesley, completed a business course and then fulfilled the premedical requirements. He worked for a time at the Southern Publishing Association, where he had the reputation for searching out those who were sick and nursing them. One Friday afternoon he came home, weary and frustrated. "Mother," he said, "I want to study medicine." Eventually the way opened for him to enter the College of Medical Evangelists, where he was graduated in 1921.

As Dr. Magan continued to bear his administrative responsibilities on the Madison campus, relations between the church organization and the self-supporting institutions became more difficult. On February 28, 1911, Dr. Sutherland received a letter from the editor of the *Review and Herald* stating that inasmuch as the Madison enterprise was not under the direction of the conference, no notices or articles concerning the Madison school would henceforth appear in the church paper. This was a blow to the public relations of the institute and a discouragement to the founders who had endeavored to follow the blueprint of Christian education for the needy Southern field. In May the situation became so acute that the doctors were invited to Washington, D.C., "to meet with the brethren." Elder Evans, president of the North American Division, said, "If those men [Sutherland and Magan] were not Christian men, they never would have stood the amount of abuse which they have had to endure during the past eleven years, and I want to get them to Washington now and make peace."

For three days the committee studied the problems pertaining to the work in the South, and drafted a "peace program." The problems of a decade were not solved so quickly, and the founders continued to face many dark, discouraging hours. It is not to be wondered that Dr. Lillian was "blue," or that Dr. Percy preached on "trouble" and recorded in his diary: "Felt my own remarks. . . . [It] looks as if God were going to 'empty me from vessel to vessel.' "

When Ellen White died at "Elmshaven," July 16, 1915, Dr. Percy suffered the loss of a counselor, friend, and defender of truth, whom he had known for almost thirty years. He would miss her words of courage and her inspiring personal messages as well as her testimonies to the church.

9

A Medical School in the West

While the Nashville Agricultural and Normal Institute was struggling into existence in Tennessee in 1905, another institution was opening its doors in California. In May of that year, John A. Burden, supervisor of the sanitarium work in southern California, having been urged by Mrs. White to search for a property in the vicinity of San Bernardino and Redlands which could be used for sanitarium work, discovered a sixty-four-room institution with other buildings on seventy-six acres of land at Loma Linda. This property, originally a hotel, had been remodeled into a health resort by a group of doctors and businessmen, at an overall cost of $155,000. The project had not been a success, and the syndicate was anxious to dispose of the institution. Eager to see the medical work of Seventh-day Adventists established in this particular area, Mrs. White urged the immediate purchase of the Loma Linda property for the attractive sum of $38,500. With her encouragement, a few men of faith, led by Elder Burden, arranged the purchase and obtained the necessary finances to meet the payments as they fell due.

October 1 found the first workers on the grounds preparing the buildings for occupancy, and on the twelfth of that month the first patient registered. Loma Linda Sanitarium opened officially on November 1, with a staff of thirty-five doctors, nurses, and helpers. At the beginning of the next year a school of nursing was started with Dr. Julia White as director, and seven students enrolled.

While those who led out in initiating the work at Loma Linda had in mind the operation of only a sanitarium and a nurses' training school, Ellen White early declared, "This place will become an important educational center." Then in December she wrote further: "In regard to the school, I would say, Make it all you possibly can in the education of nurses and physicians."

The attention of the church was called to the West to find a solution to the problem of creating a medical education for its youth. The American Medical Missionary College, which had once served the young people of the denomination, was now a private institution, soon to disappear. When an Adventist youth attempted to enroll in the average medical school, he was faced with classes on Saturday.

A group of interested church members gathered at Loma Linda on April 15, 1906, with the purpose of creating educational facilities in connection with the sanitarium. The buildings were dedicated, and Mrs. White, one of the principal speakers, urged the constituency to envision the medical evangelism that could be accomplished by educated, dedicated youth. On September 20, the College of Evangelists, as it was first called, was declared officially open; however, only part of the faculty were on the grounds and there were no students! A second opening was attempted on October 4, with President W. E. Howell, the faculty, and thirty-five students on the campus.

The plans for the school did not at first envision the training of physicians, but as term followed term, the program moved in that direction. Little realizing what was involved in establishing a medical school, Elder Burden, chairman of the Loma Linda board of trustees in 1908, wrote: "You will notice from our plan that we have in mind to develop the medical school here sufficiently to qualify physicians to practice under recognition of the state. As yet we have few students who are taking the medical course direct."

By 1908 the College of Evangelists was offering three courses: evangelistic medical ("designed to qualify workers with all the ability of physicians to labor, not as physicians, but as medical missionary evangelists"), nursing, and ministerial. Dr. George K. Abbott was now the president, Elder Burden, Bible instructor, and George McCready Price, librarian and science teacher. Three sanitarium physicians—Drs. Julia White, Cora Abbott, and J. R. Leadsworth—were also on the faculty. Seven or eight students were taking the first year of the medical course, and wondering if the second year would be offered.

Trustee Burden, upon requesting the state requirements for a medical school, was told by officials that it "must conform to the requirement of the Association of American Medical Colleges; and that its building, laboratories, equipment, and faculty must meet rigid inspection."

Discouraged by the accreditation requirements for a Class A medical school, the General Conference Committee, in June, 1909, passed a resolution restricting Loma Linda to "a special training school for medical missionary workers." With unflagging determination, Elder Burden urged the board to apply for a state charter authorizing a full-fledged medical college. His efforts were rewarded when the General

Conference Committee at the Autumn Council session recommended that the Loma Linda board apply for such a charter. On December 9, 1909, a charter from the State of California was signed and recorded in Los Angeles, which authorized the college and gave it power "to grant such literary, scientific, and professional honors and degrees as are usually granted by literary, scientific, medical, and dental or pharmaceutical colleges, and particularly the honors and degrees of Bachelor of Arts, Bachelor of Science, Doctor of Medicine, Doctor of Surgery, and Doctor of Dental Surgery, and in testimony thereof to give suitable diplomas under the corporate seal."

WHAT KIND OF MEDICAL EDUCATION?

But a charter did not answer the question: What type of medical training shall be offered? Young Adventists wanted a curriculum that would help them meet the standards of the medical profession; but conservative church leaders, aware of the financial and scholastic demands of operating a medical college, opposed any course of study except a practical training without the granting of a recognized degree. When the matter came up for consideration at the session of the Pacific Union Conference held in January, 1910, Mrs. White was asked by three churchmen to give her views concerning the aims and standards of the school. She wrote: "We must provide that which is essential to qualify our youth who desire to be physicians, so that they may intelligently fit themselves to be able to stand the examinations required to prove their efficiency as physicians. . . . The medical school at Loma Linda is to be of the highest order, because those who are in that school have the privilege of maintaining a living connection with the wisest of all physicians, from whom there is communicated knowledge of a superior order. And for the special preparation of those of our youth who have clear convictions of their duty to obtain a medical education that will enable them to pass the examinations required by law of all who practice as regularly qualified physicians, we are to supply whatever may be required, so that these youth need not be compelled to go to medical schools conducted by men not of our faith."

Elder I. H. Evans, the General Conference representative present at the conference, declared: "When the statement from Sister White is read, I am sure that the majority of our brethren will feel as we feel tonight—that the Lord has spoken, and we will obey."

When the proposal was presented to the delegates, unanimous

action was taken to make the school at Loma Linda a full-fledged medical college. In May a council was called in Loma Linda to unify the organization of the school and to consider methods of financing its expansion. By this time the institution was supported by all union conferences west of the Mississippi and the Lake Union Conference. On May 11 the Articles of Corporation were drawn up which consolidated the sanitarium and medical school under the legal name "The College of Medical Evangelists."

The board elected Dr. W. A. Ruble president of the college, and instructed him to strengthen the faculty. It also voted an appropriation not to exceed $35,000 to construct a hospital and a dormitory, and to purchase necessary equipment. The president began a search for qualified physicians who would join the C.M.E. teaching staff. He invited Drs. Newton Evans, George Thomason, W. H. Holden, F. M. Rossiter, and others in England and Australia to become members of the faculty. However, the college could not make attractive offers, as President Ruble's letter to Dr. E. H. Risley reveals: "I might say that physicians are accepting a salary of $20 a week. This is the most that is paid to anyone." Not many responded.

On September 29, 1910, exactly ten days after Percy Magan started the medical course at the University of Tennessee, the College of Medical Evangelists was officially opened as the "denominational medical school," with twenty-four freshmen and ten sophomore medical students. The cottages which served as dormitories were bulging, with three or four students to a room. There were problems, too, in the operation of the anatomy laboratory. The sanitarium management did not want the dissection of cadavers on the campus for fear it would react adversely on the patients. Therefore a laboratory was set up in the second floor of a building in Colton, a town five miles away, and students rode local trains or walked to Colton to do their dissecting.

MEDICAL EDUCATION IN AMERICA

During the first decade of the twentieth century medical education was inadequate and inferior in the majority of American medical colleges. Of the 150 medical schools operating in 1905, only a few were giving what today would be considered an adequate type of training.

In 1908, Dr. Abraham Flexner was requested by organized medicine and the Carnegie Foundation for the Advancement of Teaching to conduct an investigation of American medical education. He accepted the assignment and visited over 150 institutions. His report focused public opinion on the tragic deficiencies of the majority of the schools. As the result of his survey, the worst ones were closed, and a constructive program of improvement was made in those that survived.

At this inauspicious moment for new medical institutions, C.M.E. sought accreditation. Dr. N. P. Colwell, Secretary of the Council on Medical Education of the American Medical Association, visited Loma Linda soon after the school was incorporated. With the current plight of medical education in his mind, the secretary held out little hope that the school could meet the higher standards. He declared that it was the avowed purpose of the medical profession to crush the "one-horse medical schools." Nevertheless Dr. Colwell sympathized with the aims and purposes of C.M.E., and the school was granted a C rating by the American Medical Association.

THE CHURCH IS PERPLEXED

In 1910 few Seventh-day Adventists comprehended what was happening in medical education in the United States. They saw little need to pour money into the construction of classrooms, laboratories, and hospitals. Church leaders knew of many physicians who, by taking short courses, had received the M.D. degree. Furthermore, it had been possible for a young man to be trained in medicine by any physician who would act as his preceptor. Some argued that the young people should take short courses in medical evangelism, as they did in ministerial training, to prepare them for foreign-mission service.

Therefore, when high standards of training were suddenly demanded, and when adequate laboratories and hospitals were declared essential for C.M.E., leaders in the North American Division balked at appropriating the funds called for to carry on a medical college.

The laboratory building, authorized early in 1910, had not even been started a year later. The president of C.M.E. expressed his discouragement bluntly: "It is getting quite desperate with us here. We hardly know what to do." The work was delayed for lack of money, and conference presidents waited for "a more convenient season."

By the middle of 1911, however, there were signs of progress. The laboratory was under way, additional land adjoining the campus was purchased, and several more doctors joined the faculty. Since clinical facilities were inadequate in the area, Dr. Ruble envisioned the day when the fifth year of study (for the course was five years) would be conducted in Los Angeles.

RAISING THE STANDARDS

If C.M.E. was to serve the international church, it must receive the highest accreditation in America and overseas. The handicap of a C rating was admitted from the beginning, since it was the mark of an unrecognized college. As early as 1913, twenty-five state boards refused to allow students from C-grade schools to take examinations. In December, 1911, W. A. Spicer, secretary of the General Conference, had reported to A. G. Daniells, the president, "We had a visit from the examining board of the American Medical Association some weeks ago. He seemed well pleased with the progress we are making, but of course expects by the time he returns in two years to find a hospital, a well-equipped laboratory, a good library, and other facilities that are necessary for a medical school. These things must be provided if we expect to have a first-class medical school."

The medical college faced a stalemate in 1912. Two years had passed since the board had voted to build a hospital, but as yet there was no money to begin construction. The clinical experience needed by students was inadequate at the Loma Linda Sanitarium and the San Bernardino County Hospital. Some students were receiving training at the Glendale Sanitarium; but President Ruble was prodding the board to open a dispensary in Los Angeles. He also looked ahead to the day when students might obtain clinical experience at the Los Angeles County Hospital. Mrs. White supported the metropolitan project. As she met with the board at Loma Linda on April 4, 1910, to study with them the solution to the problem of adequate clinical training for the third- and fourth-year students, she lent her approval for the plan which called for doing "part of the work here [Loma Linda], and part in Los Angeles."

Elder G. A. Watson, local conference president, also reports that Mrs. White, in conversation with him in Los Angeles, declared: "This city must be taken into account with our work in Loma Linda." There were organizational problems within C.M.E. concerning which areas of administration were to be controlled by the business manager and which by the president.

In 1913 the new hospital was constructed at Loma Linda, additional changes were made in the faculty, and more rigid entrance requirements were formulated for the medical course. One of the most far-reaching actions was the opening on September 29 of the Los Angeles dispensary at 941 East First Street. It was difficult to find enough doctors to staff the clinic; however, volunteers came forward and the instruction was thorough. Within a year it was necessary to erect additional rooms.

Discouragements shrouded the medical school in 1914. Some of the leading doctors had grave doubts that the institution could survive when the board met, for some of the members "had blood in their eyes and a groan in their voice regarding the Loma Linda enterprise." Fortunately, the dire consequences anticipated did not materialize.

In an attempt to increase the confidence of the church in the program of medical education, the board enlarged the constituency of C.M.E. to include the executive committees of the General Conference, the North American Division Conference, the Pacific Union Conference, and the Southern California Conference, as well as the original corporators and the medical college faculty. There was need for sympathetic understanding and a unified policy on the part of both the ministry and the medical profession. The school needed an administrator who could be a liaison officer to the medical associations of the nation. He should be a doctor who could instill courage and confidence in church members and conference leaders, for without their support the project could never succeed.

DR. NEWTON EVANS BECOMES PRESIDENT

A change of administration took place in August, 1914, when Dr. Ruble requested that he be relieved of his responsibilities, and Dr. Newton G. Evans, professor of pathology at the University of Tennessee, was elected president. Shortly after the new administrator arrived, Dr. Colwell again inspected the Loma Linda campus and the Los Angeles dispensary. "I am much encouraged at his apparent attitude toward what he has seen," said Dr. Evans.

As the new president grappled with the problems, he felt the need for assistance in obtaining higher accreditation. Dr. Evans thought of his friend in Tennessee, whom he had encouraged to take the medical course when the venture seemed foolhardy because of Magan's duties, lack of finance, and age. Dr. Evans realized that the Irishman had winning ways in public relations, that he was an astute educator who had developed in trial and sacrifice, and that he was undivided in his loyalty to the church. President Evans felt certain that Dr. Magan was the outstanding man in the church to make contacts with the doctors who controlled the medical education of the nation. His views were shared by some of the members of the board. When the Council on Medical Education of the American Medical Association met in Chicago in February, 1915, Doctor Magan was asked to join Drs. Ruble and Evans as the officially appointed committee to represent C.M.E. Dr. J. A. Witherspoon, a close friend and former teacher of Dr. Magan, had recently been president of the A.M.A., and he did what he could to prepare the way for the representatives. But the efforts of the committee were not successful, and the Council turned down the request for a B rating.* However, the contacts which Dr. Magan made were not in vain, for the friendships he started in the political circles of the A.M.A. would grow and be of inestimable value in years to come.

Although defeat was discouraging, Dr. Magan would not tolerate complacency; he strained for action. Writing to W. C. White, he said, "The B rating means doubtful; state boards can do as they please in regard to accepting it or not. C [the rating of C.M.E.] means utterly worthless." Then he told the story of a man who received a telegram which read: "Your mother-in-law is dead. Shall we cremate or bury her?" The man wired the reply: "Both cremate and bury her. Take no chances." It was the doctor's view that "no chances" should be taken in the matter of accrediting; every effort should be made to obtain an A rating.

Early in March Dr. Magan, in an eight-page letter to Elder White, a member of the C.M.E. board, outlined the results of the Chicago convention. He presented a lengthy résumé of the requirements facing the school: "I do not see that there is any way under heaven unless God works miracles whereby we can get out of this state of affairs. It

---

*Dr. N. P. Colwell, Secretary of the A.M.A. Council on Medical Education, gave the committee a full report of the weaknesses of C.M.E. in 1915, which may be summarized as follows:

1. The clinical faculty of the Los Angeles division was not satisfactory, as it depended upon teachers from other medical schools.
2. The first- and second-year courses at Loma Linda were not arranged in a logical manner.
3. The anatomy laboratory "was an insult to the college."
4. The pathology laboratory was inadequate; the course in pharmacology was weak.
5. The plan of registration and the provision for student credentials were inadequate.
6. It was unsatisfactory "to do part of the work in Loma Linda and part in Los Angeles."
7. It was imperative that C.M.E. own and control a 200-bed clinical hospital in Los Angeles.

does not seem to me, however, that this should cause us to lose interest or be discouraged. I kept telling Dr. Evans that no matter how hard things are, God would work something out for the whole experience. I have felt for a long time, and you pardon me for saying it, that Loma Linda needs a deeper experience in the real missionary spirit of sacrifice and in God's ways of healing the sick. To my mind it would be one of the worst things in the world if Loma Linda should be able to get into the legal 'A' grade and at the same time not be in the spiritual 'A' grade."

Then, with optimism, the doctor added: "I know that to many the situation at Loma Linda looks to be desperate, but frankly, Brother White, I do not so regard it. To me the opportunity of our lives for the Loma Linda medical college is before us. With self-sacrificing and devoted teachers and students rallied to the right principles, we can make the school go and the world will yet recognize the worth of our work. I believe that God is testing us whether we will stick to Him or not."

Thus at the Chicago medical meetings Dr. Magan, for the first time, faced the denomination's medical problems. Here the institution and the man met! From that day C.M.E. would never be separated from the thought, talent, and energy of this Adventist physician-educator.

10

An "Inspirator" for C.M.E.

In 1914, as officials of the General Conference evaluated the qualifications essential in the leadership of the medical school, they sought a man who was a physician, educator, promoter, diplomat, and a minister with heart religion. Soon they turned to Dr. Magan at the Madison school. In the summer, Elder E. E. Andross, president of the C.M.E. board, and Dr. Newton Evans arrived in Nashville to talk with Percy about connecting with the institution. In the autumn, Elder White followed up the talk of the two officials by writing to his friend: "The more I study the difficulties arising in the minds of our students regarding the Loma Linda medical school, the more I feel that we must have in Los Angeles a strong leader and teacher. . . . I told our brethren at the board meeting how I felt about the requirements of the work in Los Angeles, and I also told them that I thought your experience and your natural abilities provided in you many of the qualities of leadership, and faith, and missionary zeal, and economy, that would enable you to do a great work with limited facilities. And therefore I thought you ought to be approached with the proposition that you go to join the Loma Linda faculty, and take the leadership of the work at Los Angeles."

Dr. Magan's reply to the proposal was not enthusiastic. He wrote: "In the first place I have but little confidence in myself as an organizer and leader. This may seem strange to you, knowing as you do all the experience I have had in this kind of work. But the tremendous needs of this kind of work, and the problems to be grappled with appall me as I think of them. I am not much of a reformer. I do not lead out in daring reforms. If I am certain that the spirit of prophecy points in a certain direction, I ask God for grace to lead me and give me strength to follow in the light. But without this I make but few moves."

Evaluating the needs of the school, the physician-educator gave his blueprint of what should be done. "Again, if I were to be connected with Loma Linda I fear I should want to inaugurate some radical changes," he admitted. "I have some very definite ideas in my head concerning the conduct of a Seventh-day Adventist medical college. I firmly believe that it ought to get into the Association of American Medical Colleges, but it never can get a better rating by the way its matters have been handled in the past. Our appeal will have to be made on an altogether different basis."

Dr. Magan was convinced that the students at Los Angeles "need an 'inspirator' more than an 'educator.' They need to be welded to this message. . . . My medical experience is small and amounts to little, but I have the acquaintance of a number of the leading men in the American Medical Association, and these men have a great respect for us. . . . But they will not be reached by an attempt to copy worldly models and standards, but rather because they respect us for the kind of work we are endeavoring to do, and because of our missionary spirit and enterprise."

Dr. Magan was invited, with the representatives of the Southern Union, to attend the 1915 Autumn Council of the General Conference Committee at Loma Linda. Of his plans he wrote, "It has been definitely settled that I will attend the council meeting to be held at Loma Linda. Dr. Lillian will accompany me. She has not been away from home for several years to amount to anything, and is much worn out."

When the couple arrived in the West, they saw for the first time the medical school in action. Dr. Percy visited the dispensary for clinical work at Los Angeles, and pronounced it "a rotten place." He also saw the architect's rough plans for the proposed Ellen G. White Memorial Hospital—plans that would eventually become a part of his bloodstream, of every breath he took.

THE HOUR OF DECISION

Because of its $400,000 debt, the medical school came under severe scrutiny at the council. Certain men were determined to close the institution. Writing to Dr. David Paulson immediately after the conclave, Dr. Magan said, "We have just passed through one of the biggest battles in the history of the denomination, nominally over Loma Linda, but in reality involving the integrity of the spirit of prophecy and our belief in the same." He described it as one of the "fiercest . . . contests" he had ever witnessed, and added that "if the Lord had not worked some miracles there would have been a terrible state of affairs."

When the council met at six o'clock on Thursday morning, November 18, a motion came on the floor, sponsored and urged by those who did not believe the church should or could operate a first-class medical college. Dr. Magan saw that the action would commit the school to "innocuous desuetude, or to a maximum of deadly inefficiency." The plan would force students after two years at Loma Linda to go to other medical schools to finish the course.

Several years later, in describing the speeches that were made to save the medical school, Dr. Magan paid tribute to Elder Daniells. The General Conference president arose and addressed the council, saying, "My brethren, I am astounded and I must speak. If I do not say my mind I will be a coward and unworthy of your confidence. Brethren, listen to me. We all profess faith in the spirit of prophecy, but we forget that one of the last things the prophet ever wrote was that our young men and women should be given their full training in our own school and should not be forced to go to worldly schools. And here we are, before the prophet is hardly cold in her grave, proposing that our young men and women shall only have half their education from us and then shall be turned loose in these worldly schools. Now, I protest against it. That is all I can do, but I do most earnestly protest it. We can build up this school. We can support it. We can do anything that God wants us to do."

According to others who were present, stirring speeches by Elder W. C. White, Elder George I. Butler, and Dr. Magan were strong influences in turning the vote in favor of a fully accredited medical school. From his firsthand experience, Dr. Percy told exactly what Adventist youth would face in a typical medical school. "His words were so pointed and took such a deep hold that men who strongly opposed the continuance of the school were practically unable to answer Magan's arguments, and those who were battling for the school took a new grip." The full four-year medical course was maintained; the College of Medical Evangelists was saved.

The leaders of the denomination, taking into account the involvements, were now committed to the operation of a medical college. They would stand by it and make it succeed.

A week after the meeting of the council, on Thanksgiving Day, November 25, the board elected Dr. Magan to be dean of the Los Angeles division of the medical school. The position was not made particularly attractive to the physician, who had already started a successful private practice in Nashville along with his educational work at Madison. Dr. Newton Evans explained that when the new dean was elected, "objection was made to the expenditure of the extra money which would be needed to meet his salary." Therefore he was invited to join the faculty on the condition that he would meet "his own expenses in the work" by raising his own salary of $23 a week! This was a serious handicap; he was burdened with a personal debt, for he had borrowed hundreds of dollars to assist himself through his medical training.

HANGING IN THE BALANCE

When Dr. Magan joined the staff of C.M.E., he found that, in the eyes of the secretary of the Council on Medical Education, the school lacked "a complete and solid organization." Before the Autumn Council at Loma Linda, Magan had observed that there was a spirit of defeatism among church leaders at Washington, D.C. "Most of the brethren around here seem to feel it is useless to try to meet the A.M.A. standard," he observed. "I do not think that any of them have any really clearly defined view as to what the province of Loma Linda Medical College in this old world ought to be. God will have to raise up some men with a vision, who will put that thing through in the face of great opposition."

Refusing to be defeated by discouraging circumstances, Dr. Magan asked, "Has it come to this, . . . that Seventh-day Adventists are going to decide what they have power to do or not to do upon the statements of men who are not connected with God or His precious cause in the earth?" Then he continued: "If we had listened to the counsel of worldlings, I do not suppose we ever would have started our schools, our sanitariums, our publishing houses, and our magnificent organizations and enterprises of this people, all of which have grown out of very feeble and very imperfect beginnings, started, however, in the fear and under the hand of a mighty God, according to the word of His servant, the prophet."

As he undertook his work as dean of the medical school, he set forth three points to be faced in evaluating the future of the institution: First, if plans to gain the highest accreditation for C.M.E. were dropped, the American Medical Association would have no confidence in future attempts of the church to establish such an institution. Second, since God had told the church that men of power and influence would aid the medical-missionary program, the leaders should go forward by faith. Third, if the church turned back from establishing a medical college in harmony with the spirit of prophecy counsel, the youth of the denomination would lose faith in that counsel.

THE VETERAN CAMPAIGNER

Within a week after he joined the medical school faculty, Dr. Percy plunged into a campaign to help raise $61,000 for the hospital in Los Angeles; and by December 15, 1915, he was able to give the board a progress report. He encouraged the women of the church who, under the direction of Mrs. S. N. Haskell, had requested that they might raise funds for the project. He also urged that the name, "Ellen G. White Memorial Hospital," voted by the board on June 17, be adopted officially as a tribute to the messenger of the church. There was some opposition to the name, but when the General Conference polled the field leadership the ratio for its approval was about three to one.

As a veteran campaigner for funds, the dean now set out on trips to every section of the country to solicit money and pledges for the hospital. He visited colleges and sanitariums, called on men and women of wealth, rode a handcar and a freight train in Vermont to see prospective donors, and pleaded with conference officials—all for the medical college! In medical terms he described his attempt to obtain a donation from a wealthy church member: "I am trying to perform a major surgical operation upon her pocketbook which, I trust, will help her spiritual metabolism."

Though naturally optimistic and courageous, Dr. Percy was almost crushed again and again by the mountains of difficulty that towered over the medical school. In the center of a busy program he was lonely, for he wrote his friend, Dr. Sutherland, confessing, "I miss you very, very much. Somehow or other I find myself too old in life to form a new friendship such as yours and mine has been."

On one of his first field trips, he stopped at the Hinsdale Sanitarium to visit with his friend, Dr. David Paulson. In this quiet retreat, Magan studied the testimonies concerning Loma Linda. At this time he wrote: "I cannot but feel that in Los Angeles I have undertaken the biggest contract in my life, and I know that without special help from God it will shipwreck me, for I am not big enough, nor man enough, and I do not have sense enough to put that thing through. It is beset with difficulties from every side."

His humility in the face of difficulties was his salvation, for he realized his need for divine aid. Many are the notations in his diary of hours spent in prayer. For example, after a day of perplexing conferences at Loma Linda, he wrote: "In the evening walked round the hill to my favorite seat and prayed for a long time. God strengthened me and many things began to clear up in my mind. A sense of security in God came over me and I knew that He is my Helper."

Returning to Los Angeles from a lengthy itinerary, the dean faced almost insurmountable problems. He and the president were struggling to find qualified faculty members to teach the junior and senior students at the Los Angeles division. The American Medical Association had refused to allow physicians who taught at the University of Southern California Medical School to be members of the C.M.E. faculty, although the men were willing to serve in the dual capacity.

Furthermore, Dr. Percy could not feel the pulse of the medical college since he was not on the committee to locate the hospital (though he had to raise the funds for it), he was not on the committee to study the architect's plans, he was not on the board, and not the head of any department. He was beginning to speculate as to what dean meant in relation to the school!

THE ACCREDITATION REPORT

The board of trustees studied the report of the A.M.A. Council on Medical Education, which pointed out specific weaknesses that must be corrected before the school's rating could be raised above Class C.

Dr. Colwell gave an amazing summary of the wage scale of the C.M.E. faculty. In his survey he made this observation. "It was claimed that there are ten full-time teachers, and that the total expense for salaries amounts to $15,368. This sum, however, includes expenses for janitor service and other help about the institution. One of the full-time teachers receives $1,200 per year; four receive a salary of $1,100 each, and one receives $1,000. (Salaries for four not given.)" It might be noted that the salary rates at that time were comparable to those paid to ministers of the church.

An embarrassing situation, which could have jeopardized the school, developed when one of the nonmedical leaders in Washington, D.C., went over the administrative heads of C.M.E., and attempted to deal directly with the Council on Medical Education. Such unethical procedure might have permanently damaged the program of accreditation. It is no wonder that Dr. Witherspoon told Dr. Magan in Nashville: "Make any sacrifice to accomplish an end but don't let men tie your hand so you can't accomplish the end." The influential physician reminded the dean that the C.M.E. board had promised to improve facilities and build a hospital, but the promises had not been fulfilled. Then he warned Dr. Magan: "About one more bad report from the inspector and your name is Dennis."

Dr. Magan wrote a letter of sympathy to Mrs. Lenna Salisbury, widow of Professor Homer Salisbury, a member of the E.M.C. faculty in its beginnings, who had lost his life when his ship was torpedoed in the Mediterranean. Referring to the mission service of the Salisburys in India, Dr. Magan declared: "I meant every word that I said in regard to ending my days in India. Ever since I was there, I have always wanted to go back and labor there. . . . I sometimes think that God does not *lead me,* He *drives me*. I have no desire to stay in this country. There is such a turmoil of strife here all the time, I weary of it more than I can tell. And so many of our people and even our workers seem to have lost the old-time spirit of real self-sacrifice for this cause. I do not say this to criticize—I think you will understand me. I do not know how long I will be connected with the medical college. I have a kind of an intuition that God will use me to help get it on its feet and that after that someone else can carry on the work better than I can. I have pioneered things so long, for a great many years, and I am not happy unless I am pioneering, and again, I think my ideas of sacrifice for this truth and the humble, simple way in which God will carry on His work do not harmonize with the ideas of a great many of my brethren here. And on this account I presume also I will be free for the frontier in the course of a few years, and possibly in a less time that that."

But new frontiers would continue to challenge him at the medical school; days would come and go, and he would have no release from the problems. Perhaps the hard work of raising funds was a good tonic for him. This was a project he enjoyed, and it kept discouragement from overwhelming him in the turmoil of organizational and accreditation issues. But fund raising for the hospital bogged down as opposition continued. "I am being fought on this medical school proposition," wrote Dr. Magan, "from one end of the country to the other. . . . Opposition of every name and nature that the devil can manufacture, invent, or imagine, has been brought to bear against the whole thing; but God lives and reigns, and in spite of all this I have gathered a pledge list of over $40,000 positive pledges, and the people who pledged to me are sticking loyally. . . . We have purchased the land for the site, an entire block in the principal part of the city of Los Angeles."

STRUGGLES IN FUND RAISING

Almost in desperation President Evans wrote to the president of the North American Division Conference: "In our efforts to advance the providing of the necessary improvements in Los Angeles, I am concerned over the fact that apparently practically nothing is being done except what Dr. Magan is doing in the raising of the money. In the petition which you drew up for our board, addressed to the North American Division, the matter of appointment of solicitors and getting them into the field was turned exclusively into the hands of the North American Division Committee . . . looking to the raising of this money. . . . This was a good many weeks ago, and I do not know of anything that is being done looking to these ends. I confess it alarms me, and to an onlooker would appear as an effort not to advance this movement but to destroy it."

Accusations were made against the administrators of C.M.E. that they were allowing certain doctors in private practice to influence and control the policies of the institution. This criticism shocked Dr. Magan, and he promptly stated that no doctor had asked for or received control of any kind. "Many of them are willing to give their time free of charge in the teaching work, and we will be unable to carry on our work without them." The crisis came to a head on April 23, when the dean submitted his resignation to the board because of rumors that he was "disloyal to fundamental policies of S.D.A. institutional management" and that he was "liable to turn the operation of the Los Angeles hospital over to physicians" who were not "organically connected with our institutional work."

The resignation was, of course, not accepted; but the action awakened some of the trustees to the fact that unity and the staunch support of sound policies were necessary if the medical college was to succeed. Because of such accusations, Dr. Evans sometimes lost his courage. Dr. Magan confided in his former colleague, Dr. Sutherland, concerning the situation. He said that Dr. Evans "was terribly discouraged when I got here; in fact, he was just about ready to quit." Then he added, "But the Lord has helped me to bat some of these fellows over the head, and things are looking up."

In the spring of 1916, the dean made a decision which influenced the future of the Los Angeles division, by purchasing the entire block in Boyle Heights. The board had authorized the purchase of half the site; but more room would certainly be required. Business manager Burden agreed that if the hospital was necessary for the clinical work of the school the entire block should be purchased; but the raising of money and the completion of the deal rested squarely upon Dr. Magan's shoulders. It was necessary for him to buy the extra land in the name of a private party, gather $6,000 cash in three days, and wait hopefully for an additional $2,000 to complete the transaction. After he had received the approval of local board members, Dr. Percy went after the land, and with typical enthusiasm he announced the purchase to Elder White: "I have not told the brethren at Washington anything about it. It will be bought and paid for by friends and given free of all strings of any name or nature to the medical school corporation."

Additional sidelights concerning the purchase of the land were related later by the doctor. He said, "One morning at Loma Linda I bade Dr. Evans good-bye and told him he would not see my face again until I had money enough to buy the north half of the 1700 block [on Boyle Avenue]. . . . In a few days I had enough money to pay all the cash that was required, letting the mortgage stand for a bit. Then I went up to Loma Linda where a board meeting was called, and told the brethren that I had purchased the north half of the 1700 block in the name of Stephen N. and Hettie Haskell."

For the unauthorized purchase, Magan received an official scolding, followed by the inquiry, "What will you do with the extra land?"

"I plan to put up a building and manufacture yellow pups!" the Irishman replied, grinning.

When Dr. Sutherland heard of the many skirmishes his former colleague faced, he wrote Dr. Percy in this wise: "I expect you to fight this battle and win. And I expect you to stay there and see that thing through, and make Loma Linda a more glorious place than Battle Creek ever was." It was grand counsel from one veteran warrior to another, and Dr. Percy would need to remember it in the days ahead. It was a time for individual strength and vision in the administrators of the medical school. If courage to act had been lacking, C.M.E. would have died in its infancy!

11

Through Deep Shadows of War

On April 6, 1917, America declared war, and within three weeks Congress passed the Conscriptive Draft Act, making all men between twenty-one and forty years of age eligible for military service. Between the declaration of war and the enactment of this draft law the General Conference in Spring Council, at Huntsville, Alabama, April 12-19, framed "a carefully worded declaration," setting forth the denomination's attitude on war. In part the pronouncement stated: "We believe that civil government is ordained of God, and that in the exercise of its legitimate functions it should receive the support of its citizens. We believe in the principles upon which this Government was founded. We are loyal to its Constitution, which is based upon the principles of democracy, and guarantees civil and religious liberty to all its citizens. . . .

"We have been noncombatants throughout our history. . . . We petition that our religious convictions be recognized by those in authority, and that we be required to serve our country only in such capacity as will not violate our conscientious obedience to the law of God as contained in the Decalogue, interpreted in the teachings of Christ, and exemplified in His life."

Because of the hysteria of the times this church memorial to the Government was not received sympathetically by the public. In his travels through the country shortly after America entered the war, Dr. Magan found "very, very strong prejudice against us as a people because of this memorial." He said further in a letter: "Undoubtedly the brethren worded it the best they knew how, but for some reason or other, it seems to have been grossly misunderstood, and the papers in Washington, D.C., New York City, Chicago, and other large towns, have criticized us unmercifully over it." Dr. Magan wished that "a tone of more warmth and loyalty and offerings of service of certain kinds to the Government" had been emphasized.

Theodore Roosevelt bitterly attacked conscientious objectors, and Dr. Magan said, "It is quite generally understood that he means Seventh-day Adventists more than anyone else." When Dr. Percy talked with Dr. Franklin H. Martin of Chicago, who had been appointed by President Wilson as a member of the Advisory Commission of the National Defense, he found him prejudiced against Adventists because of their stand on the war. After the dean had explained the actual position of the church, Dr. Martin became cordial. He outlined the needs of the Army for 28,000 doctors—with only 3,000 in sight—and he urged the administrators of C.M.E. to consider forming a base hospital unit, staffed entirely by Adventists, which would stand ready for overseas duty.

Back in Los Angeles the war emergency prodded the board to act on the school's expansion program. With the block of land in Boyle Heights purchased, the new Los Angeles dispensary in operation, the dormitories for women and for men nearly completed, some men urged that work be started on the hospital building.

A DEVOTION FOR HIS STUDENTS

During the spring of 1917 Dean Magan remained close to the campus in a busy round of teaching and counseling. This was the work he loved most, for he said, "I have a deep burden for the students at Los Angeles. They are like sheep without a shepherd down there, scattered from one end of town to the other. They have no one who is fathering or mothering them or endeavoring to hold their interest for this cause. If they get away from us and become worldly in their ideals, we will never forgive ourselves, and God has given me a burden to help them along these lines. This lies very near to my heart."

But the change in the nation's way of life soon forced him to start on a hectic period of travel, conducting interviews and meeting committees in the East and the Middle West. Wartime transportation was an ordeal that tried the most patient traveler. Passenger service was sidetracked for troop and supply trains, and accommodations deteriorated rapidly as the months passed. Since the nation was sending millions of tons of grain to the Allies, food conservation—called "Hooverizing" after Herbert Hoover—was in evidence everywhere. In the dining cars there were placards to remind the guests to conserve food. Bread was served only upon request, and then it was likely to be dark bread, made of rye, barley, and oats. Food portions were cut a third in size, but prices seemed to rise in ratio to the decreasing amount on the plate.

By the first of July the pressure of war had produced a number of acute problems in the church. Dr. Magan promoted the calling of an emergency council, held at Loma Linda, July 3 and 4, to discuss the proposed base hospital, food conservation, first-aid classes, and the drafting of medical students and faculty members, as well as other problems concerning the school and its relation to the Government.

Recounting the happenings at the session, he wrote: "Dr. Sutherland was called upon to present the food question, and it was enthusiastically voted that we recommend to the North American Division that the denomination establish a food commissioner, and that we organize the denomination for food conservation work the country over. . . . I was asked to present the matter of the base hospital, and it was unanimously voted that we organize that."

FACING DELICATE ISSUES

On July 13 the dean left home, thinking that his principal business in Washington, D.C., would be to offer the services of the school in organizing a base hospital unit to be set up in France. However, he received a telegram from President Evans warning him that the future of the medical college was at stake, since all students and doctors were subject to the draft.

Dr. Magan plunged into the wartime turmoil of the nation's capital, where he interviewed important Government officials. When he consulted Dr. Martin, whom he had seen two months earlier, the dean found that the only hope to keep medical and premedical students in school was to rush the names of any who were drafted to the Secretary of War in the hope that they might be exempted. Faculty members would be considered by the Council on National Defense, and those who were absolutely essential to the conduct of the school would be urged to join the Medical Reserve.

The plan for a base hospital, if and when the Government needed it, was finally approved. The offer was never accepted by the Army, but the action changed the attitude toward Adventists in some Government circles.

While Dr. Percy was in Washington, he arranged for several Adventist leaders to meet with Herbert Hoover to discuss the food conservation program. Some of the General Conference officials were opposed to any contact with the Government; but after long discussion they agreed to send a small delegation to keep the appointment. When the churchmen gathered in the office, Mr. Hoover's secretary called upon one of the ministers to offer prayer. (This minister had been violently opposed to the visit. When the secretary had asked Dr. Magan whom he would suggest to open the conference with prayer, the doctor had diplomatically suggested this "reluctant" brother!)

Mr. Hoover told the Adventist leaders of the famine-stricken multitudes which the commission was helping, and he pleaded with them to support the food conservation program which would save millions of lives in Europe. Again, such contacts, engineered by Dr. Magan, helped the leaders of the church to gain a broader vision of the service God wanted His people to perform in a war-weary world.

By the first of August, 1917, the draft boards were taking medical students at a rapid rate, and C.M.E. administrators wondered how many would be left to enter classes when the term opened in September. Every medical school in the nation was in jeopardy, since no provision had been made for interns or medical students to continue their training. On the last day of August the school received a telegram from Dr. Martin, stating: "A REGULATION PROVIDING FOR EXEMPTION OF INTERNS AND MEDICAL STUDENTS AUTHORIZED BY PRESIDENT."

The Supplemental Regulations of the Government stated that "hospital interns who are graduates of well-recognized medical schools or medical students in their fourth, third, or second year in any well-recognized medical school who have not been called by a local board may enlist in the Enlisted Reserve Corps, . . . and if they are thereafter called by a local board, they may be discharged on proper claim presented on the ground that they are in the military service of the United States." Furthermore, the same group could, if they had been called by their local draft board, seek discharge from military duty to obtain enlistment in the Enlisted Reserve Corps.

THE ORDEAL OF ACCREDITATION

When C.M.E. opened in mid-September, some twenty freshmen medical students were enrolled, although there was no draft exemption for this group. However, the President's ruling for advanced medical students and interns seemed to ensure the continuance of classes. But on October 1, President Evans was informed by Surgeon General of the Army W. C. Gorgas that students who had sought a discharge in harmony with the national directive had been refused exemption. When the reason was sought, the Surgeon General explained that the Army refused exemptions to schools whose graduates were not accepted by 70 percent of the state boards, and that C.M.E. was "not recognized by 50 percent of the state examining boards."

Drs. Evans and Magan realized that the medical college faced the most serious ordeal in its short history. If the school were closed in this crisis, it would never have an opportunity to reopen. President Evans summarized the situation: "Six of the medical students, four sophomores and two seniors, have already gone to American Lake. Five other boys from Loma Linda and the nurses' training school have also gone. According to the list that I have, there are thirteen of the medical students altogether who are in the first draft and who are not exempted; this includes the six who have already gone. How many others of these thirteen will go and when they may go seems to be an uncertain matter at the present time." In Los Angeles, Dr. Evans interviewed Dr. William R. Molony, president of the Board of Medical Examiners, who sent a telegram to Senator Hiram Johnson, protesting the C rating of the medical school and urging consideration for students called by the draft.

When the disastrous announcement came, Dean Magan had immediately entrained for Washington, D.C., in an effort to win Government recognition through the assistance of Army officers, physicians, and church leaders. There were interminable delays, however, since key figures, such as General Gorgas and Major Vaughn, the doctors who had the final decision on the medical schools to be recognized by the Army, were not in their offices.

When Dr. Percy learned that the exemption of C.M.E. students depended upon a higher rating of the school, he hurried from Washington, D.C., to Chicago, where Major Vaughn and Dr. Martin were attending the Clinical Council of Surgeons. Dr. Magan remembered that Dr. George Hare, of Fresno, president of the American Academy of Medicine, was a close friend of Major Vaughn, and he wired Dr. Evans to bring Dr. Hare, a strong supporter of C.M.E., with him to Chicago. When the two doctors arrived from the west coast, they joined Magan in a series of conferences that lasted for days. Dr. Hare prepared a survey of the student scholarship record of C.M.E. for the three previous years, which revealed a steady improvement. And one of the facts that eventually helped to overcome prejudice was the record of one graduate who had received the highest grade of any applicant at any examination during that year. Finally, on October 25, Dr. Colwell, secretary of the Council on Medical Education, and Dr. George H. Simmons, general secretary of the American Medical Association, sat down with Drs. Hare, Evans, and Magan.

"We have had a meeting and have talked your matter over," said

Dr. Simmons. "I have settled what is going to be done about the College of Medical Evangelists." Then he added, "I want someone to go to Washington for me."

"I will go, sir," said Dr. Magan.

"All right. You be in Major Vaughn's office at ten o'clock Monday morning," said Dr. Simmons.

"Yes, sir, I'll be there."

"And you tell him I want the College of Medical Evangelists raised in its rating immediately!"

"Yes, Dr. Simmons," said the Irishman.

"And if Vaughn doesn't do what you tell him to do, you get on the telephone and let me know. I'll settle it!"

As Dr. Magan later recounted the critical interview he added, "Little did I think of the many times I would go to that same office with a wonderfully different standing than I had in that fateful hour."

On Monday morning Drs. Hare and Magan were face to face with Major Vaughn, a potbellied little man, almost humorous to see in his uniform.

"Gentlemen," he began, "I don't know what's up, but I've been snowed under with telegrams about your school in California." Then he added in Army style, "You know, I don't think that school is worth a ——"

"It's a better school now, Vaughn, than yours was when you were dean at Ann Arbor," cracked back Dr. Hare. "You didn't know enough then to analyze sputum."

"Well, George," said the major to his old friend, "I guess you're right; but what am I to do?"

"Do exactly what the old man [Dr. Simmons] tells you, Vaughn, or something will happen quick."

"I guess you're right, George, I guess you're right," said Major Vaughn. "Now what will we do?"

"If you'll excuse me, Dr. Vaughn," interjected Dr. Magan, "I suggest you put all the pressure you can from General Noble, Colonel Love, Surgeon General Gorgas, and your own prestige, to make the A.M.A. raise our rating."

"That's the thing to do," said Major Vaughn enthusiastically. "We'll do it!"

The three men went to Surgeon General Gorgas's office, and although he was away they filed into the office where the two military men, General Noble and Colonel Love, stood. Major Vaughn spoke: "I want to introduce Dr. George Hare and Dr. Percy Magan," he began. "I've told these gentlemen that if they will get their school raised into the B rating we will cancel all orders for their students going to the Army and let them finish their course so that they can serve as medical officers. Is that satisfactory?"

"Yes, Major, yes," said the two officers.

"That's settled, then," declared the major with a sigh of relief. As the men turned to leave, a redheaded sergeant standing by the door spoke to Dr. Magan. "I know you've been having a difficult time, sir," he sympathized. "But I could do a lot for you if you will give me the name of every medical student called in this draft. I'll see you get them back."

When the dean gave the sergeant the names, he said "We'll get the wires going right now." And he did!

Thus the Army accepted the reclassification of the medical school subject to the report of the Council on Medical Education, and Dr. Colwell promised to make the inspection visit within two weeks. "The tide has turned in our favor," was the way Dr. Percy expressed it. He sent a barrage of letters and telegrams to the management and department heads of C.M.E., urging them to be ready for inspection. "There must be no fooling about this," he wrote. To F. W. Drake, superintendent of new construction, the dean charged: "Spare no pains to push the work on the surgery building as fast as you can and a good deal faster. Get more men, get students to help, but get that building as near completed as you can. . . . Get that filthy crop of tin cans, rubber boots, cast-off clothing, and other elements of the abomination of desolation reaped with the sickle of the reaper and burned in your incinerator."

A TIME FOR QUICK ACTION

In the midst of the complex situation in the East, Dr. Magan did not forget minute details at the Los Angeles division. To Dr. A. H. Larson he wrote: "I wish we could get hold of a little apparatus for the eye room. . . . Also I wish we could get a few more instruments for the operating room. . . . I think it would be well, if it meets your mind, if the students could all arrange to have gowns so as to work in the clinic in their gowns regularly, and especially when he [Dr. Colwell] is there."

To Dr. Alfred Shryock, at the Loma Linda division, were sent these suggestions: "Now please do your best to have everything at

Loma Linda in apple-pie order so that nothing will be awry when he comes. The hospital records should all be up in good shape, and the autopsy records also. Everything in the laboratory should be put in as good condition as time will permit."

One of the last letters in the series was addressed to L. M. Bowen, business manager. After the varied instructions given in other notes, the dean touched a spiritual chord when he said: "The Lord has worked miracles for us thus far, and I do not want to see things fall down now through any fault of ours. You remember that expression in *Prophets and Kings*: 'God can work miracles for His people only as they act their part with untiring energy. He calls for men of devotion to His work, men of moral courage, with ardent love for souls, and with a zeal that never flags. Such workers will find no task too arduous, no prospect too hopeless; they will labor on, undaunted, until apparent defeat is turned into glorious victory.' "

Dr. Colwell inspected the school thoroughly, and he said good-bye to Dr. Magan with the promise, "I will do my utmost to secure the raise in rating for you." The next day, November 14, the dean received the telephone call he had long awaited. Dr. Colwell announced to him that C.M.E. could be assured of the Class B rating.

Jubilant over the victory, Dr. Magan telegraphed the Surgeon General, asking the return of the drafted medical students. Then he sent telegrams and letters to all of the young men in the Army camps. Among other things, the weary but happy dean said, "I cannot at present write you a long letter, but I think I can truthfully state that I have spent the longest and hardest seven weeks of my life in trying to get you your rights under the ruling of the Surgeon General of the United States Army in regard to students in good standing in medical colleges."

Before the soldiers could have received the letter, this telegram brought them sunshine: "DR. COLWELL HAS BEEN HERE AND HAS RAISED OUR RATING TO B GRADE. COUNCIL ON MEDICAL EDUCATION WILL CONFIRM. TELEGRAM ALREADY GONE TO SURGEON GENERAL RELATIVE TO YOU. . . . LETTER FOLLOWS. LEAVE MATTER IN MY HANDS, AND KEEP CONFIDENTIAL. WILL RUSH MATTERS AS FAST AS POSSIBLE. NOTIFY THE OTHERS."

While there was rejoicing on the Los Angeles and Loma Linda campuses, Dr. Magan could not forget the seven weeks of suspense and struggle. More than twenty years later he recounted to the C.M.E.

constituency the tense days when he walked with God by faith: "There is something about the experience of having the burden of a great crisis rolled upon you when you are alone which drives you very close to God. I was on my way to save the only medical school in all the world which bore the name of God. Practically speaking, I knew not one soul there, not a man in the office of the Surgeon General. I felt to pray the prayer of Martin Luther which had for years appealed to me: 'O Thou, my God! Do Thou, my God, stand by me against all the world's wisdom and reason. . . . For myself I would prefer to have peaceful days, and to be out of this turmoil. But Thine, O Lord, is the cause.'

"From office to office and from one great man to another I went, but nowhere did I get a word of comfort. I remember one bitter cold day, with driving wind and snow, disheartened and not knowing what next to do, I left the office of the Surgeon General and sat down on the stone curbing supporting the iron fence around the White House. There I sat and prayed, and there came into my mind some of the closing words in Solomon's great prayer at the dedication of the temple—'and let these my words . . . be nigh unto the Lord our God day and night, that He maintain the cause of His servant.' . . .

"I remembered the prayers which so often fell from the lips of Ellen G. White, of John Burden, of many another soul who struggled to launch the school. I, too, had prayed and it came into my mind that prayers do not die when they leave our lips; they are 'nigh unto the Lord our God day and night.' I knew that the prayers offered long ago were still doing duty before the great white throne, and I was comforted."

New Year's Day, 1918, was designated as Jubilee Day, and at Dr. Magan's suggestion the celebration was held in the afternoon on the Loma Linda campus. Invitations went out to faculty members and their families, to members of the Loma Linda Church and other churches in the area, and to the staff members of Glendale Sanitarium and Paradise Valley Sanitarium. "A free dinner for students, nurses, visiting doctors, and special guests was the feature of the day." The church was decorated with ferns and flowers, while an orchestra played music in a "triumphant mood." Speeches were made, and a thank offering was received. All of the boys except one had returned from the Army camps, and they related some of their experiences.

THE DEDICATION OF THE HOSPITAL

The dedication of the White Memorial Hospital in Los Angeles on Sunday afternoon, April 21, brought a crowd of over 2,000 persons to Boyle Heights. In the midst of the open-air program, while Dr. Magan was speaking, a heavy earthquake swayed Southern California. The Irish wit of the doctor reacted in the emergency, and he reminded his friend, Dr. Holden, "that it takes a good-sized man to make a speech that will start an earthquake!"

As the Los Angeles division progressed, Dr. Percy was happy to inform Dr. Colwell of the more stable financial program voted by the board. The General Conference had made an annual grant of $50,000, and authorized a $35,000 building program, which would include additional classrooms, laboratories, a chapel and assembly hall, and additional patient rooms to bring the capacity to 135 beds.

Aroused by the thorough inspection that was to be made by the Council on Medical Education in all medical schools in the nation, the board pushed a dynamic program of building and equipping the medical college. "If we can get into the A grade," said Dr. Magan, "then our cause is settled forever, that is, as long as God wants our people to prepare medical missionaries for the world. I have now been urged to complete this plant as rapidly as I can get hold of money. The brethren want me to put up the building which will contain classrooms, kitchen, dining rooms, and laboratories at once. I am doing everything in my power to get money for this. I have also been urged to put up the building for the maternity and children's hospital."

WILL THIS END C.M.E.?

But suddenly the outlook changed, and the school faced its worst crisis. By the middle of July Dr. Magan learned of the new wartime status of medical colleges from Colonel Arnold. The education program was being streamlined throughout the country as medical-school teachers were called into the Army. Schools in which the class and clinical work had been carried on in two places were required to consolidate. This ruling would force C.M.E. to concentrate all of its work in Los Angeles.

While the Army desired to help medical students remain in training, yet C.M.E. now faced more serious complications. "The general plan for protecting the medical students," explained Dr. Percy, "is to have them join the volunteer training corps of the different colleges where they are enrolled. These volunteer student training corps make the men enlisted soldiers in the Army, and they are under control of a military officer, and there must be 100 of them in each school which has such a unit, and the 100 must be of a college grade." Neither Loma Linda nor the Los Angeles division of the school had a training corps or any plans for such an organization.

The war brought an upsurge of freshmen students to Loma Linda, and by the end of August over forty-five applicants had been accepted —almost two and a half times as many as any previous first-year class. By September the Army draft situation had worsened, and Dr. Magan saw that the school was heading into rough weather. Dr. Ruble, now secretary of the General Conference Medical Department, discovered that the Army would recognize only those medical schools that offered the Student Army Training Corps (SATC). It seemed that C.M.E. could remain open only by moving to Los Angeles and forming a unit for its students.

Immediately a series of conferences, telegraphic communications, and committee sessions were set in motion by the school administrators. Since Dr. Ray Lyman Wilbur, president of Stanford University, was director of SATC units in California, Dr. Magan sought his friendly cooperation. But the leading church officials in Washington, anxious to maintain the noncombatant status of the Adventist youth, were fearful that a training-corps program would jeopardize the position of the church. Therefore the medical-school group decided to seek the cooperation of Redlands University to train Loma Linda students in its unit, while Los Angeles students could join the Occidental College unit. They would drill for six hours each week without surrendering denominational principles.

Successful arrangements to guarantee the continuation of C.M.E. were almost completed when the administration received a telegram from the General Conference, refusing to allow the students to join SATC. The churchmen explained that they were afraid of compromising the noncombatant status of the denomination, although it was admitted that students would have no military training and they would not be called to Army service until they had completed medicine and were full-fledged physicians. A telegram signed by Elder J. W. Christian, president of the board, and four other members was sent to the General Conference: "YOUR WIRE HAS CAUSED US DEEP PERPLEXITY. BOARD MET. WITH ALL

COURTESY BELIEVE YOU ABSOLUTELY MISUNDERSTAND SITUATION IN WHICH YOU PLACE US. MAJORITY MEDICAL STUDENTS ALREADY IN RESERVE CORPS WHICH IS TO BE SUPERSEDED BY STUDENTS' ARMY TRAINING CORPS. FOLLOWING YOUR COUNSEL SCHOOL MUST CLOSE IMMEDIATELY. WE HAVE INFORMATION THAT ONCE CLOSED IT WILL NEVER BE PERMITTED TO REOPEN. OFFICIALS WITH WHOM WE HAVE COUNSELED HAVE ASSURED US THAT NONCOMBATANT STATUS WILL NOT BE COMPROMISED BY TRAINING CORPS IN MEDICAL SCHOOL."

There would be no actual compromise, as Dr. Magan viewed the issues. "None of our medical boys get to France, or into active service where they wear a uniform, carry a trench knife, or anything else," he declared. "They are simply on the inactive list until they finish their medical course, and then they go in as surgeons and carry nothing, and I never heard of a surgeon being armed in the Army. There might be some excuse for the brethren's position if our medical students went overseas in the enlisted Medical Reserve Corps, but they do not do that. The only way they get over is when they are out of the enlisted Medical Reserve Corps and are commissioned surgeons in the Army, and I do not believe that any of our good brethren will yet take the position that a man ought not to be in the Army as a surgeon."

Since the influenza epidemic had sent Dr. Magan to bed seriously ill, Dr. Evans went to Washington, D.C., to see if there was any way to save the medical school. On October 31, he believed the condition to be hopeless. The General Conference could not see how the Government's plan could operate at Loma Linda or Los Angeles, and there was no alternative.

The chaotic situation on the campuses may well be imagined. Students were restless as draft boards went into action on their cases. Some students endeavored to transfer to other medical schools to continue their education. The issue was summed up in another telegram sent by Elder Christian and Dr. Magan to Dr. Evans while he was still in Washington: "BELIEVE IT VITAL TO FUTURE WELFARE OF DENOMINATIONAL MEDICAL WORK YOU ALL FIND SOME WAY TO AVOID CLOSING SCHOOL AND TURNING STUDENTS TO THE WORLD."

But the General Conference and the board of C.M.E. found no solution. Only divine intervention prevented the collapse of the medical college—a collapse which would have ended the denominational medical-education program for all time!

The Armistice was signed on November 11. The war was over. The hour of relief did not come a moment too soon, for five of the students were to entrain for Army camps that very day. Dr. Magan, who had done all he could to save the school, had seen every human effort fail. Now he gave thanks for God's overruling act. "Personally, I feel deeply grateful to a kind heavenly Father that just as our perplexities were reaching such a crisis, in His mercy He brought this war to an end," he said humbly. "Over and over again I think of those words in *Prophets and Kings:* 'He who slumbers not, who is continually at work for the accomplishment of His designs, will carry forward His work. He will thwart the purposes of wicked men and will bring to confusion the counsels of those who plot mischief against His people. He who is the King, the Lord of hosts, sitteth between the cherubim, and amidst the strife and tumult of nations He guards His children still. When the strongholds of kings shall be overthrown, when the arrows of wrath shall strike through the hearts of His enemies, His people will be safe in His hands.' Certainly God did cause the strongholds of kings to 'be overthrown' just at the moment when things looked so dark for us, and thus fulfilled His word, 'He guards His children still.' . . . God certainly heard our prayers, for hardly a student in the end was taken. Five were summoned the day before the war closed, but when they went to entrain they were ordered back to the school."

But Dr. Percy was not satisfied with the success of the moment. With vision for the future, he began planning to meet such a crisis if it should ever be repeated. "I have been thinking earnestly and praying earnestly over the whole matter of our medical school," he declared, "and I am inclined to think that we can take some steps in reorganization now during the little time of peace that will better the case for our medical students and put them in a place where they will be treated by the Government as ministers and missionaries if such treatment is accorded at all, which I very much doubt it will be when the next war begins. However, it is worthwhile thinking about, and we must do everything possible to guard our institutions and our youth."

12

The End of the Long, Long Battle

The six years following the Armistice (1919-24) saw Dr. Magan in a whirl of varied activities that would have sapped the strength of two ordinary mortals. With no private medical practice, the dean spent his time, as he described it, organizing and expanding the school, gathering funds, economizing, praying with students, and urging them to prepare for denominational service.

After the influenza epidemic of 1918, which swamped the hospital's facilities, the administrator plunged into the never-ending task of money raising. A goal of $16,500 was set to complete projects on the Loma Linda and Los Angeles campuses. Since the major portion of the funds was allotted to Loma Linda, the Jubilee headquarters were set up there. By April, 1919, the dean could report over one third of the amount "in sight." Dr. Shryock designed a goal device which Dr. Magan described to Dr. Evans, who was doing graduate work in the East. "I have gotten a large scoreboard on a little grass plot that the autos turn around on in front of the sanitarium at Loma Linda," explained Dr. Percy. "It is 12 x 16. There is a beautiful gold frame around it; [it is] painted green, and marked off [with] silver linings, and we have an affair over the top which throws beautiful electric-light beams down on it at night. The names of our different teams are arranged on one side, and the daily score for every day through the month of May . . . will be recorded thereon. The whole Loma Linda Hill is aflame to go over the top in this matter. It is great fun if it does not kill us all to do it."

No source of cash was neglected in bolstering the campaign treasury. When Dr. Holden of Portland, Oregon, was unable to accept the invitation to give the commencement address, he offered to donate money equal to the cost of the trip. "I am not so sure but the $100 would be worth more to the school than my spiel," he said. "If you think so, let me off and I will give you the $100."

"Agreed, Billy," replied the dean. "We let you off. Please send me the $100 and do it quick. We are trying to have all the money in by June 1, the date of graduation, when we expect to have a Jubilee."

The campaign ended victoriously on June 1, with the college commencement exercises in the evening as the climax of a happy day. Into the wee small hours of the next morning worked the campaign committee, counting cash and pledges. Then, with less than four hours of sleep, Dr. Magan was up and on the highway driving to Los Angeles, though he did admit, "I feel like the morning after!"

There was always the need, however, for more funds, and the trustees looked to the versatile Irishman to produce a large share of the money from special friends of the school. On one occasion, however, the treasurer of the General Conference suggested that the dean obtain money for a project "without a direct appeal to our people or an appropriation from the conference." Dr. Magan replied in his spirited style. "That, while I know it was not intended so, sounds a little like the order of the ancient Ramses to the children of Israel to make bricks without straw, and this old sinner is hardly that brilliant yet."

ADMINISTRATIVE PROBLEMS

There was a never-ending procession of administrative problems across the dean's desk, and in the perspective of time, some of them seem ludicrous. C.M.E. had struggled for years to get enough qualified students enrolled in its classes; but now, as medicine became a more popular profession in the denomination, the college enrollment increased. When the freshman enrollment of 1919 soared to fifty, some of the board members clamored for a 50 percent cut to ward off an overproduction of doctors.

There were misunderstandings, too, concerning the placement of graduates. Naturally the General Conference was anxious to see more physicians going to foreign countries for mission service; but the attempts on the part of the school to get volunteers who were ready and willing to serve were often frustrated. Dean Magan set forth the situation from his perspective in a letter to Dr. Sutherland. He explained that "practically everyone we tried to get into the work" was turned down either for "lack of funds" or with the excuse that "no medical help is needed" in such and such a field, or "nothing can be done until after the Fall Council." The administrator determined to keep pushing young doctors to volunteer for medical-missionary service until the denomination would devise plans to use every one of them. Writing to the president of the General Conference, Dr. Magan said, "I fully appreciate that you are limited in your operations along the lines of medical work and foreign missions, and I also appreciate that it will be necessary for the young men and women who graduate from this school to have a spirit in them that will make them willing to go anywhere, work with anyone, and do anything that they may be asked to do, and I am doing everything in my power toward this end."

A little later, when critics of the school spoke out in Autumn Council, Dr. Evans arose and read off the list of graduates, showing that "65 percent were godly medical missionaries." This report "closed the mouths of those who had been criticizing and finding fault," reported Dr. Magan happily.

Medical education took a strange turn in southern California in May, 1919, which Dr. Magan described fully. "It was my lot," he said, "to sit in the meeting of the Council of Medical Education of the Association of American Medical Colleges and listen to a resolution being solemnly read and unanimously voted upon to expel the Medical Department of the University of Southern California from the Association of American Medical Colleges on the ground that their work was overpoor, their equipment worse than nothing, and the dean of their college utterly oblivious to the needs of the hour. This scene was somewhat dramatic to me, for Dr. Charles Bryson, the dean of the Medical Department of the southern California university, has been one of the most bitter and sarcastic enemies that this school has had. He has done everything that he could to injure us in every way possible. His students have scoffed at our students; but we have lived to see the day when he has been publicly humiliated, and now it looks as if his school was going to pieces. While his school was being treated in this way, our school was receiving all kinds of kindly recognition and invitations to join different medical associations, et cetera. . . . Our dispensary has grown now until it is the largest in the city and is generally considered to be by far the best organized and equipped. . . . The greatest physicians of the town, good men, honest men, who respect us and love our principles, are now very anxious to get on our staff."

GRADUATING U.S.C. MEDICAL STUDENTS

A year later the University of Southern California Medical School closed its doors, leaving its students without the opportunity to complete their course. In April, 1920, faculty and students of the defunct school waited upon the C.M.E. administrators, petitioning them to accept their seniors as special students who would complete their studies at C.M.E. but receive their diplomas from the university. Dr. Magan telegraphed Dr. Colwell for counsel. In the message he said: "WE ARE WILLING TO FAVOR THOSE WHO ARE DESERVING, PROVIDING IT WOULD NOT JEOPARDIZE OUR STANDING WITH YOU. JUDGE CAN HANDLE THEM WITHOUT INJURY TO OUR STUDENTS."

The Council on Medical Education saw no objection to the plan if the seniors met the requirements, and if the clinical faculty was adequate to handle the increased enrollment. Dr. Percy assured the Council that a high standard of teaching would be maintained, particularly since the entire facilities of the Los Angeles County Hospital were now available to C.M.E. and a new fifty-bed unit of the White Memorial Hospital offered additional clinical facilities. "I am sure you will realize next time you make us a visit," wrote Dr. Magan to Dr. Colwell, "that although we are far from being perfect, yet we have made tremendous strides since you were here last."

When C.M.E. received its charter there were five other medical schools in Los Angeles, but by 1920 all of them had closed their doors, leaving only the small, unendowed Seventh-day Adventist institution. Not only had it survived, but the entire clinical facilities of the metropolitan area were available for its faculty and students. Officials of other medical schools had attempted to discourage the Adventist leaders by saying that it was impossible for them to establish a school without millions of dollars in endowments. But C.M.E., built by the faith and sacrifice of its constituency, was growing, and its facilities were expanding.

With the opening of the 1920-21 term, C.M.E. had seventy freshmen at Loma Linda, and the facilities were crowded in Los Angeles with the addition of thirty-four senior and junior students from the University of Southern California Medical School. To arranged classrooms, lecturers, and clinical facilities was a strenuous task, but the dean was certain "that we will be able to do some good to some of the students."

The reaction of the "adopted" students from U.S.C. was excellent. They felt "that they would have been down and out medically if it had not been that a helping hand was held out to them by the Adventists," explained the dean, "and we were the only people who did hold out a helping hand to them. Physicians in the town, especially their old teachers, feel that we have been their friends."

When Dr. Magan visited the offices of the Council on Medical

Education in the autumn of 1920, he found Dr. Colwell enthusiastic about the future of the school. The years of friendship between the two men had created a confidence and a mutual understanding that assured better days ahead for C.M.E. "Well, Magan, I feel ashamed of myself sitting here rating you people, which is a little bit of a job, while you are doing the really big things of the world," said Dr. Colwell with sincere admiration. "You have done wonders in your school, and I am proud of you; and while you have not converted me to the seventh-day Sabbath as yet, you have converted me on practically everything else about your medical work."

"A FLAME IN THE HEATHER OF ISRAEL"

In the spring of 1921 the hopes of the faculty and board were high that the accrediting committee would raise the school to an A rating. On May 15, Dr. W. E. Musgrave, Superintendent of Hospitals of the University of California, Heartley F. Peart, General Counsel for the State Medical Society, and C. J. Sullivan, Executive Secretary of the League for the Conservation of Public Health, inspected the institution. While the committee was sympathetic with the aims and objectives of C.M.E., its findings, known as the Musgrave Report, pointed out serious weaknesses and defects in the institution. When the report was received and studied, there was bitterness, disappointment, and pessimism on the two campuses and in Washington, D.C. "Sometimes I feel most disheartened," admitted Dr. Percy, "when I think of all the hard toil we have put in here to build up something worthy of God's name in the earth, and then to have our rating held up because of certain . . . policies."

What were the findings and recommendations of the inspection committee? One of the most serious defects centered in the organization of the administrative and business departments. The business manager was the chief executive officer of the board, which arrangement, in the eyes of the examiners, made "the president of the faculty and the dean subservient to the business manager."

The divided campus of the school did not promote unity of action or strength in medical education. Dr. Musgrave said: "The division of the school, partly at Loma Linda and partly at Los Angeles, does not invite the highest degree of efficiency, but in my opinion an organization could be drawn that would allow them to continue to use both locations, as they obviously must, not having room enough in Los Angeles for the entire school without material decrease in efficiency. Obviously, the real headquarters of the school must be located in Los Angeles. This must be made the heart of the institution and the plant at Loma Linda must take secondary place."

Recommendations included the enlargement of the medical library, the increase in teaching personnel, the appointment of an executive committee of five or seven members of the board to correlate and carry out policies and actions, and an increase of at least 25 percent in the budget.

The Musgrave Report was "like a flame in the heather of Israel," said Magan, and soon there were hectic committee sessions of available board members and the school administrators. The dean was not particularly perturbed over the storm clouds, since he had weathered many a squall. So he expressed his opinion in his inimitable style: "I think they had an idea that they were going to squash us pretty quickly. They wanted to be good and treat us right, but they were firmly of the opinion that I had written the Musgrave Report. They might just as well have accused me of having written President Harding's inaugural address. I had exactly as much to say to one as the other. . . . We were together from six in the morning until ten at night, never even stopping for dinner, with the exception of three-hour routine board meeting in the afternoon. . . . There was a big demand made on me to show the original Musgrave Report which Musgrave wrote Colwell. This I absolutely refused to do unless Colwell and Musgrave will release the report. . . . Now if these men are so anxious to read what he had to say about them, I am sure I am willing. We can't be in a tougher place with them than we are, and I know Musgrave will stand by me to the finish." Referring to his need of self-control in the stormy sessions, Dr. Percy declared, "I had to use my dove end and squelch my serpent end!" In spite of the differing views in councils and committees, the Irishman loved and honored his brethren. He once said that he did not wish to deprecate the church leadership, for "these men in spite of faults in regard to the operation of our work [C.M.E.] are certainly the chosen servants of God."

Feeling that the American Medical Association was attempting to dictate how the college should be run, the frustrated board refused to consider the Musgrave Report. Since it was "not inclined to do anything at all" about the recommendations, it postponed the issue for many months. This did not disturb the dean, who stated frankly: "As far as I am concerned, from one standpoint I care but little. I have worked like a slave ever since I have been here, and my sole desire, as far as the school is concerned, is to put it where the Lord would have it, and to make it the light in the earth He designs it shall be. We have been told by the spirit of prophecy that we must work in harmony with 'the legal requirements' of the state and the nation in the matter of training our young physicians. It seems very difficult for these men to get this matter clear in their minds. . . . One thing certain—if they refuse to do the thing which the Council on Medical Education and Hospitals of the American Medical Association request them to do, the school will be closed, for the American Medical Association will simply shove it down into the C Grade."

Although Dr. Colwell encouraged Dr. Magan to have faith in the future, saying that if the school "makes all the changes" suggested it could eventually expect to receive the A rating, yet when he made an inspection early in 1922, he was forced to admit, "The Council endorses the findings in the inspection made by Dr. W. E. Musgrave on May 15, 1921, acting for the Council. The corrections he suggests are of extreme importance and particularly the one urging the centralization of control in the dean or president of the school of medicine."

In the spring of 1922 the board finally faced the recommendations and voted to reorganize the school in harmony with the findings of the Committee. By April Dr. Musgrave could report with a touch of subtle humor to Dr. Colwell: "The trustees of the school have now, after very mature deliberation, done what to them was a very monumental piece of work, in approving the organization we recommended to them. I feel that they should now be recognized as a Class A school, and I so recommend to you." In May the constituency gave final approval to the reorganization program, although two items were yet to be carried out.

Dr. Musgrave's letter of recommendation was presented by Dr. Colwell to the Saint Louis session of the Council on Medical Education. The majority of the members urged that another survey be made by the Council's regular inspector before the rating was actually granted.

The medical school rolled out the red carpet for Dr. Colwell when he arrived on November 3. After he had toured every nook and corner of the institution from boiler room to dormitories, he was taken to a luncheon in his honor given at the Athletic Club of Los Angeles. About fifteen leading physicians of the community were present, and after these men—including Dr. Granville MacGowan, surgeon and organizer of the Los Angeles Health Department—had spoken, Dr. Colwell arose and addressed them. In recounting the speech, Dr. Magan wrote:

"He [Dr. Colwell] began something like this: 'There is one part of Dr. MacGowan's speech to which I can most heartily agree, namely, that part in which he said that when the Seventh-day Adventists first started, how that from the beginning, a number of us felt that they were doomed for defeat. I told them over and over again not to make a start. But today I must confess that their faith has triumphed over my unbelief. Some years ago Dr. Magan took me over the place which their hospital plant now covers. It was then a mass of weeds, cockleburs, and there were two or three sorry-looking animals feeding upon it. Dr. Magan remarked to me that someday we would have a great medical institution there. I thought to myself: You poor soul, you do not know what you are talking about, you will never be able to have a first-class medical school; but today I walk over that same block covered with beautiful buildings, and veritable hive of medical activities. I have not completed my inspection yet, but I am almost certain as to the kind of report I will make, and I am sure you will all be satisfied with it.' "

On November 16, 1922, Dr. Colwell sent Dr. Magan the official statement: "After watching the efforts you have been making to develop your medical school during the past several years, it is my most pleasing duty to inform you that at its business meeting on November 14, the Council on Medical Education and Hospitals voted that the College of Medical Evangelists be granted a Class A rating. Considering the manner in which improvements in the past have been made, the Council voted this high rating, fully confident that the places which are still comparatively weak will be strengthened, and that the institution will continue to improve."

The years of struggle for accreditation were now history; but the man who had contributed the most, who had endured when others gave up the fight, was humble in the hour of victory. "Well, this ends the long, long battle," said Dr. Percy. "As I look over it, I think it has been one of the greatest in my life. . . . Surely the hand of God has been over this place, and over and over again have the hearts of men been turned from their set and studied purposes against us, so that they have become our warmest friends. I can never feel thankful enough to our heavenly Father for all of His kindness, and I am praying daily that the experiences through which we have passed may ever have an influence to keep the hearts of our dear young men and women turned toward the great God who needs their service in this world's lazar house of sorrow."

To the General Conference Dr. Percy could sum up the official news of accreditation in a poignant understatement: "Thus endeth that chapter which has been a long and dreary one."

The A rating made the school's graduates eligible to take the examinations of the National Board of Medical Examiners, and, if successful, they could practice in most states without taking additional examinations. Furthermore, doctors who held diplomas from the National Board of Medical Examiners were eligible to take examinations in Great Britain, which saved a year of extra study previously required of C.M.E. graduates going into mission service in British countries.

13

The Kindly Irishman

While Percy Magan moved in the limelight as a doctor, educator, administrator, and troubleshooter, yet "offstage" he was a man of versatile interests, a devoted father and husband, and a constant friend. In spite of the busy routine, he fostered the art of friendliness. In his relationships with fellow travelers on life's highway he was ever thoughtful of their desires. He philosophized that "the making and keeping of friends" was a rich asset, and that "we make friends by being good to those who have been everything else but that to us."

Thoughtfulness is one of the chief ingredients for making friends, and Dr. Percy had this. It was his rule "that everything outside of advertisements that comes into the office must be answered." This might include a note of appreciation to the owner of the garage that serviced his car, to whom he could say, "I know of no better set of mechanics or nicer group of men in their lines than the men who work for you." Or when a demure little miss sent him a thank-you card, written in childish script, the administrator took time to write: "Dear Carolyn: I am glad you enjoyed your Easter and had a good time. I worked hard all day, but in the evening a gentleman and his wife came over to our house and spent the evening with us, and we had a nice time. . . . Now I must say good-bye, and I hope you will have a very happy summer." Three nurses who acted as waitresses for a special dinner received this thank-you from the dean: "This little note is to express my deep appreciation of the kindly and ladylike manner in which you waited upon the table for the meeting of the General Hospital Board last Friday. The doctors were all very pleased. . . . Thank you all very, very much."

Writing to a C.M.E. alumnus whose little daughter was seriously ill, Dr. Magan gave this bit of philosophy: "Sorrows come to all of us in life, some more and to others less. After all they are our kindest friends and our best teachers. I have often thought that if all the sorrows were taken out of our lives there would be very little religion left in our lives. It is hard for us to know and understand what is best."

When tragedy struck a friend, there were always words of sympathy and courage from the physician. When an alumnus buried his wife in far-off Hong Kong, Dr. Magan wrote: "I cannot tell you what a terrible shock it was to me to learn of the death of your dear wife. . . . I only wish, my lad, I could say something really worth-while to comfort and cheer you in the sad loss which has come into your life; but how little there is that one poor man can say to another under these circumstances. I have been through it."

When an alumnus died, Dr. Magan, as the sympathetic minister, wrote the bereaved wife a comforting letter. He said, "I can only pray, dear daughter, that God will bless me with thoughts that are deeply fervent and words that are reverently earnest so that I may be of a little comfort and consolation to you in this hard hour.

"Tragic and heart-rending is your grief; nevertheless I cannot help but ponder over the fact that you have much for which to be thankful. I once read an expression from Sir James Barrie, a great Scotchman and at one time rector of St. Andrews University, in which he said, 'God gives us memories that we may have roses in December.' I have thought of that over and over again and you, my dear child, I know must have many, many precious memories of your married life. . . .

"These things are very, very hard to understand, but I often rejoice to think that the Great Book has told us that now we see through a glass darkly, literally as in a riddle, but then face to face; now we know in part, literally we know a little of much; but then shall we know even as also we are known. All of this tells us that to understand all the things that come to us in life is not our lot. . . .

"I will close with the simple prayer that He who has said that not a sparrow falls to the ground but your heavenly Father knows, and that the very hairs of your head are numbered, will comfort and bless you, and fulfill to you the measure of that great promise which He wrote down so long ago, 'I am the God of the fatherless and the widow.' "

The bitter experiences of his boyhood, his loneliness that came with separation from loved ones and home, helped mold the doctor into a true humanitarian, who was ever sympathetic with the sorrows of others. He admitted that his early experiences had influenced his outlook on life when he said, "It may be that I would never have had the inclination that I do have to try once in a while to lighten the burden and sorrows of others if my own life had been set in a different mold. . . . As a lad in my bitterness I somehow always had a desire to give my life to helping souls whom others did not want to help. I do not think it is any credit to me. Maybe it was a kind of vengeance more than godliness, but people who are in sorrow and trouble always appeal to me, and I am thankful that they do."

BRIGHTENING THE PATH FOR OTHERS

In his office interviews, whether with a senior medical student harassed by debt, or a nurse provoked by an inconvenient work schedule, Dean Magan gave each visitor his undivided attention. He kept his desk cleared of papers in order that he would have no temptation to divert his mind to other matters during the conversation. He remembered the wise counsel of Ellen White, who once said to him, "Brother Magan, always do whatever you can to brighten the path of people in such circumstances, for it may be the last kindness that will ever be done them here on earth."

Expressions of appreciation are another attribute of a friendly person, and Dr. Percy was adept with a sincere word of praise to friends or relatives. Thirty years after his Battle Creek College days he wrote Miss Ida Rankin, thanking her for the generous assistance she gave him when he was a "sick and lonely" newcomer on the campus. "I have often felt," he declared, "and have many times said to others, that I owed you a great deal of the credit for whatever little blessing I have ever been to others, or whatever little success I have made of my life."

Frequently the wisdom of Solomon was needed in making decisions on the campus. One afternoon Dr. Magan received an urgent telephone call from the supervisor of nurses asking him to come and help her solve a grave emergency. The maternity ward had sent a baby home with a Jewish mother and father; it had then been discovered it was not their baby. The parents, convinced that someone was trying to steal their child, refused to return it. With skillful diplomacy, Dean Magan sent the couple away happy with their rightful baby, and then he did his best to calm the distraught supervisor.

Once it was the dean's duty to meet an emergency in the hospital's maternity ward because the cries of patients in labor were disturbing the neighbors in the vicinity. How he solved the situation is not recorded! When told of certain happenings in a junior class meeting, the dean did not reveal his informer. He simply said, "I learned it from the mother of the deceased Unknown Soldier."

The medical fraternity knew and respected this Christian physician. They elected him vice-president of the Los Angeles Medical

Society, and he was for many years a member of the Los Angeles County Hospital board. In 1921 he was elected first vice-president of the California State Medical Association, and his circle of intimate friends in that society and among the administrators of the American Medical Association enlarged with the passing years. Because of his friendship with Dr. Percy, Dr. Ray Lyman Wilbur, president of Stanford University, agreed to be a commencement speaker at C.M.E. Another friend of the Irishman in the field of education was Dr. Rufus Von Kleinschmid, president and later chancellor of the University of Southern California. The two men had many memories to exchange, since the jovial president of the university had attended Battle Creek College for a year.

In every section of the country Dr. Magan had a host of friends. In church centers, such as Lincoln, Nebraska, Berrien Springs and Battle Creek, Michigan, Washington, D.C., and Madison, Tennessee, his acquaintances were numerous, for the links went back to college days or to his years of teaching. After years at C.M.E., the doctor visited interns, graduates in residencies, or alumni in practice in every state, and he affectionately called them "my boys and girls."

Friendship with Elder and Mrs. Heber H. Votaw and Dr. George Harding II, relatives of President Warren G. Harding, made it possible for the Irishman to have an unusual experience on one of his visits to the national capital. Through Mrs. Votaw's arrangement, he was taken through the Bureau of Printing and Engraving by the superintendent of the establishment. When the extended tour was completed, Dr. Harding and a friend called at the Bureau to pick up Dr. Magan in an official car from the White House. He described his experience, which, though he hated to admit it, actually delighted him. "When we were through, the President's Pierce-Arrow with all the regalia of office drew up to the door and your humble servant was driven in state to the White House with Drs. Harding and Mayo," he wrote Dr. Lillian. "We were most reverently treated by the traffic cops, and something of the feeling of what it must be to be a real swell laid hold upon me. Bowing flunkies, military aides, and other chaps of various ranks and sorts ushered us into the White House, and I soon divined that my stock had risen immensely since I called there a humble and unknown private citizen in the morning. After this somewhat laughable farce, Dr. Harding and I again rode the Presidential Pierce-Arrow to Takoma Park."

From the day he boarded his first train at New York for the Middle

West, Dr. Percy was to become an inveterate traveler. He knew the best and poorest of accommodations from firsthand experience. The necessity to economize sent him to railroad officials for special courtesies, and after he was an administrator, several railroads issued annual passes to him. But like other travelers who have had these concessions, he learned the truth of the saying that "dog trains for pass holders is their rule."

The advent of the automobile captured the man's imagination. Before he owned a car, as already recounted, he rode a motorcycle to Nashville from Madison to attend classes at the medical school. But the modern auto was a necessity and a pleasure for Dr. Magan as well as for his sons as they grew to manhood. The entries in his diaries reveal numerous mechanical difficulties he encountered with the cars during and after World War I. Later, as improved models came on the market, he was intrigued by their beauty, speed, and comfort. Speed, however, was one of his weaknesses, and he was stopped times without number by officers of the law. In the days of old, when eloquence could cancel many a traffic ticket, the doctor was adept at talking his way out of a fine. In later years he carried a city police badge with pride and satisfaction, which helped alleviate his traffic problems.

His classic experience with a motorcycle officer, however, was recounted on many occasions, and Dr. Percy's version of the incident went as follows: "I did tell a cop once when he stopped me for speeding that I was going to a prayer meeting. He looked at me very quizzically and replied, 'Well, Doc, if you are going to lead a prayer meeting, for goodness sake, step on the gas and go on, for every doc needs to attend prayer meeting. God bless you, Doc, and go on.' This got into the Los Angeles papers, and they had a long article about the little redheaded cop stopping me. It was near Cucamonga that the incident occurred. The paper told how that the cop had had every kind of an excuse, from borning babies to dying women, but that the prayer meeting was a new one, and he was so nonplussed that he told the doctor to step on the gas and go on. They added as the moral, 'Whoever you are, rabbi, horse thief, or doctor, it pays to be honest and go to prayer meeting.' "

THE TIES OF THE FAMILY

Dr. Percy was loyal to his family, but he often sacrificed his love of home for the advancement of the medical school. On his extended trips there was scarcely the break of a single day in his letters to his wife. If, because of the pressure of conventions or committees, he was forced to miss his daily epistle, the next day brought a humble apology. Perhaps his devotion to his wife after twenty-five years of marriage is best summed up in his own delightful way:

"Dr. Lillian is well and getting very fat," he wrote. "It is becoming to her, and her hair is silvery white and she looks very beautiful. In view of the fact that she only weighed ninety-four pounds when I married her and she tips the scales now at 135 pounds, I think I have been quite a good husband to her, but I want to tell you now, Miss Macey, she is a mighty fine-looking woman these days. Also if the good Lord had told me that I could make a woman to suit myself for my wife, I think I would have told Him, 'You need not worry giving me that permission, I will take this little creature You have here.'"

The sons came in for their share of paternal love and counsel. Wellesley and his wife Katherine moved to Covina shortly after his graduation from medicine in 1918. Shaen married Marie Young-Clarke on October 24, 1921, a few months after he completed his medical course. Then the two brothers opened medical offices together in Covina and built successful practices. Drs. Percy and Lillian frequently visited in the homes of their sons and daughters, and scarcely a week went by after the children arrived that Grandmother and Grandfather did not drop in for a few hours or stop overnight on their trips to or from Loma Linda.

The father always enjoyed shopping for his sons and his wife. One of his favorite shopping centers was Marshall Field's department store in Chicago, and on almost every visit to the Windy City he purchased gifts of clothing. When Shaen was attending the university at Memphis in 1917, the father arrived for a short visit and took his son to the clothier for much-needed attire. Shaen wrote his mother: "Dear old Dad certainly is liberal with us boys. He took me in the clothing shop and said, 'Now, Son, you get anything you want.' Mother, you know there are very few fathers who would say that to their sons. Most of them are grouchy about getting clothes for their offspring and think that they are such a big expense, etc., and grumble every time they have to shell out for anything. You don't know how much I appreciate the way you and Father treat me, and I can never thank you all or do enough for you."

On another occasion the doctor viewed the shopping for his youngest son in a somewhat realistic light: "Went to town with Val and broke myself buying clothes and shoes for the rascal."

In later years the Magan sons bestowed their love and appreciation on their parents in many tangible ways. When Dr. Percy left for the East on wearisome trips, Shaen presented him with a Pullman ticket for a restful compartment in place of the open berth he would otherwise have had to occupy. The two young doctors thrilled their father in 1932 by giving him a Cadillac, which he described to his sister in Ireland as "a beautiful vehicle, eight cylinders, very powerful, and comfortable to the nth degree." On the meager denominational salary, the senior Magans had not enjoyed many of the comforts or luxuries of life; but with the help of their sons some of these came their way in their sunset years.

On one of his trips, Dr. Magan read the life of Winston Spencer Churchill. The dedication, signed with a nom de plume, reminded him of Dr. Lillian and he wrote that it "fits another right honorable lady very well." Then he copied the passage in his letter to her:

" 'My Lady:

" 'The wife of a great man resembleth the custodian of a work of art, in that the pleasures which she derives from his company are conjoined with the responsibilities of curatorship. 'Tis hers to ensure that he enjoy health, happiness, comfort, leisure, and repose, without which provisions he cannot compass his public duties. She must be ready to accord him praise for his achievements, both large and small; sympathy in his misfortunes, even those infinitesimal; and a patient audience at all times. What a task is this, beside which his triumphs are as shadows! Not to assert—for this way exaggeration lies—that the stature of great men dependeth wholly from their wives, I yet hold it for certain that, without them, many great men would be much diminished figures.' "

The mutual love of Dr. Percy and his wife grew richer through the years. Once, after thirty-five years of marriage, the return to a hotel in Lincoln, Nebraska, sent a flood of memories through his mind. To Dr. Lillian he wrote of heaven's goodness to him and how God "led me to *you,* my own and dearest wife, who has been so good to me these long years, . . . God bless and bless and bless you!"

14

The Fighting Irish Spirit

In the midstream of the twenties, C.M.E. continued to develop under the leadership of Drs. Evans and Magan. Although the teaching program was strengthened and laboratory facilities were expanded to serve a maximum enrollment of one hundred students in each class, yet the administrators were faced with definite weaknesses in the scholastic program. Officials of the American Medical Association pointed to certain phases of instruction that needed strengthening, including better laboratory and research equipment. Teachers in a school with a divided campus needed more contact with one another and greater unity of endeavor. The students "are not being trained sufficiently well in what constitutes acceptable practice of medicine," said the report. "The facilities are there; the personnel is there."

Dr. Magan was constantly alert to changes in medical education. He was pleased with the Mayo Clinic system of handling patients and keeping records. He endeavored to put C.M.E. in the lead by unifying the clinical faculty, correlating the work, and developing new teaching techniques. "I am more and more convinced," he said to Dr. Evans, "that you are quite right that we must plan new things —progressive things in our courses of study." After surveying one Eastern medical school, the dean reported that it was conducting a strong program of clinical teaching. "They seem to have a faculty whose members make the teaching of medicine the real business of their lives. That is what we need."

The rising standards of education were also reflected in the results of a survey of students coming to Loma Linda. It revealed that many freshmen had not received a strong premedical course, particularly in science subjects, and that the liberal arts colleges needed to improve their scholarship. In 1925, when certain sincere church leaders pressured Dean Magan and the faculty to accept students with less than two years of premedical training, the administrator minced no words in analyzing the weakness of the proposal. "We have endeavored to labor very patiently and faithfully with the poorer class of students in our school," he replied candidly. "This is not the way things go in the great schools of the world. For instance, the University of California does not begin to accept into her medical college all of those who have passed their premedical work in the University. She enters only about sixty or sixty-five, and by the time the course is finished, this number is cut down to from forty to forty-five, all others having been eliminated because their scholarship was not satisfactory to their instructors. Stanford University accepts only thirty-five of the very best students from her own premedical course. . . . Now, 'we are all brethren.' We cannot weed students out in this drastic way. Our conscience could not stand for it. Our people would not stand for it. We, of course, are obliged to do some weeding, where it is manifestly clear that there is no chance of a student ever making it. But the percentage of our classes which is weeded, is very, very small, possibly three, or four, or five percent at most. . . . At the mid-summer California State Board examination, 6 percent of our students failed; none of the students from the other two medical colleges failed. Six percent is a very large percentage to fail in the home state, and affects our rating materially. . . . We have practically no great educators or doctors on our faculty, and this point is being continually thrown up to us. We are treading on thin ice as far as the laws of these great associations are concerned."

THE ACCREDITATION OF LIBERAL ARTS COLLEGES

The medical school, with Dr. Magan in the role of a persistent gadfly, may be credited with the sharp prods that moved the denomination to raise the standards of the liberal arts colleges. Not only had Ellen White in 1910 clearly indicated that the church "must provide that which is essential to qualify our youth who desire to be physicians" to stand the qualifying "examinations required by law," but she had in 1913 called upon the colleges of the denomination to recognize the "legal requirements" which made it "necessary that medical students shall take a certain preparatory course of study," urging a preparation to "carry their students to the point of literary and scientific training that is necessary."

But the response was slow. If the Irish educator had not continued to dramatize the seriousness of the issue of accreditation, the colleges might have operated indefinitely in a mediocre status. As far back as 1920, Dr. Colwell had warned the trustees that the medical school should draw its students from colleges whose premedical course was recognized by accrediting boards (such as the North Central Association of Colleges and Secondary Schools), or the standing of its graduates would be jeopardized. Dr. Percy carried on a voluminous correspondence with the denomination's college presidents, and he sought the cooperation of A.M.A. officials. Eventually, though with misgivings on the part of some churchmen, the colleges obtained junior college accrediting, which eased the situation. It was not long however, before some of the institutions decided to withdraw from the accrediting association, and it was necessary for Dean Magan to warn the boards of these colleges that such a backward step would bar their students from C.M.E. If a state of emergency developed, the medical school might find it necessary to offer the premedical course, although such a proposition was not looked upon with favor.

In 1928, denominational senior college accreditation became a major issue, and the battle waged between those who considered such recognition "unnecessary" and "worldly," and those who realized that Christian education should reach the highest standard. The college presidents placed the accreditation issue before the Autumn Council; but, as Dr. Magan described it, the issue was fought "lock, stock, barrel, horse, fŏot, and artillery!" The C.M.E. administrators pointed to the rising standards in medicine, teaching, and the other professions. Was it too much to ask Christian institutions to meet more rigid requirements? Furthermore, it was shown that the premedical course would soon be lengthened to three years and eventually to four. These added years of training would require a higher scholastic standard in every college that sent students to C.M.E. In reply, some men said that if a lack of college rating "affected the medical school adversely, the medical school could look out for itself." They neglected to consider the earnest fathers and mothers supporting these schools, whose sons and daughters were planning to be medical missionaries. Other Council delegates, however, used C.M.E. as an example of how higher standards and accreditation had in no way blurred the vision or marred the dedication to God's service of its faculty and students.

The medical college was supported in its plea by voices from all sections of the country. The Orlando (Florida) Sanitarium had been notified that its students for the nursing course must be selected from accredited colleges. California, Nebraska, and Michigan were refusing to accept students' grades from unaccredited colleges when the applicants applied for state teachers' certificates or wished to receive a degree in public-health nursing. One C.M.E. graduate who had taken his collegiate studies at Washington Missionary College "was penalized 25 percent of his premedical work . . . by the State of Minnesota and he had to make it up before he could write the State Board." Then, too, the day would soon come when the lack of accredited preparatory work would jeopardize the standing of doctors who desired to be medical missionaries in British colonies.

Through the years Dr. Magan had been conservative in his views on higher education, and he had accepted the counsel of the pioneers of the church in fostering a strong industrial program and an abbreviated college course without degrees for missionary-minded youth. This had been one of the reasons why he had urged the transfer of the college from Battle Creek to Berrien Springs. During his early years at Madison, he had openly declared that he had little faith in "higher education." But as educational standards were raised throughout the nation, the Irishman was flexible to the demands of the times and ready to meet the requirements as long as they did not compromise Adventist principles. Writing to the secretary of the General Conference Department of Education, he said, "I will give degrees and do certain things before I will ever submit to shutting our schools up, although you know that in my heart of hearts I am opposed to all that kind of stuff; but we'd better do that than to shut up altogether."

With the "long, long battle" for the A rating behind him, Dr. Percy could talk from experience with the General Conference leaders about the seriousness of the college situation. The results were gratifying, and the Autumn Council authorized the creation of a Board of Regents to develop plans for accrediting the senior colleges. Reporting the action to President Evans, Dr. Magan wrote: "It did not take Elder Spicer very long to make it known that we would soon have no schools at all if we did not seek accrediting as far as the same is at all compatible with our faith. . . . You know, the more I think of it, the more I feel assured that God has led us with His own hand in our dealings with the A.M.A., the Association of American Medical Colleges, the Scottish Board, and our own National Board, to say nothing of our relations with the State of California. We have simply endeavored in a humble manner to follow the instruction of the spirit of prophecy given us in the matter, and God hath blessed the undertaking, while our other schools have floundered around and gotten nowhere."

The church took a giant step forward in Christian education when it voted to accredit the liberal arts colleges; yet it was a slow and gradual process. From the Autumn Council of 1931, Dr. Percy sent a telegram recounting how he had talked on the floor for an hour and a half in favor of accrediting, and the Council had voted to accredit "five senior colleges." When some of the institutions found it difficult to achieve senior college rating, their administrators felt embarrassed because the junior college accrediting seemed to emphasize their weakness. With all of the delay, the medical school was placed in a precarious position. As late as 1931, *The Journal of the American Medical Association* published statistics showing that out of the C.M.E. class of 116 freshmen, only thirty-nine students were from approved colleges. Dr. Magan, writing the secretary of the General Conference Department of Education, demanded action. The national publicity of this report could do irreparable damage to the medical school. "I am deeply concerned," he said. "Prior to this the wee mutterings mentioned above have usually been to me alone. There is one little note, I think, a year ago but nothing to this. The next thing very probably will be that some medical college—not ours—will be called to order for having taken students from unaccredited schools and immediately they will ask, Why the leniency to us? The language of the prophet, whom we all loved and respected, concerning the coming of the Lord, is applicable to this situation—'Get ready, get ready, get ready.' "

When the liberal arts colleges finally met accrediting standards, they were able to give the fundamentals of Christianity to young men and women and, at the same time, qualify them to meet the requirements of any advanced education deemed essential in the carrying of the gospel to the world. Little did the churchmen of that day dream that in less than three decades the Adventist Church would establish two universities to develop the scholarship of its leaders!

DISCIPLINE MATTERS LARGE AND SMALL

At times the dean was forced to turn from the scholastic problems to matters of discipline. There were serious problems which required wisdom, good judgment, and rigidness to principle, mixed with mercy and tolerance. In addition, there were certain disciplinary items which, in the perspective of time, seem superficial. The class of 1928 must have reverted momentarily to childhood days, for Dr. Magan called a special meeting of the seniors to consider the misdemeanor of throwing spitballs and red berries in class sessions.

During this period there were strong feelings concerning the style of women's dress, and Dr. Percy was called frequently to the committee that handled these matters. Bobbed hair was a new style tabooed in most Western institutions of the church by vote of the Pacific Union Conference Committee. The medical school also took action against this style in the session of August 21, 1924, when the trustees confirmed the action of the faculty of the Los Angeles division and forbade "all women in the institution" to bob their hair. It was further voted "that those who already have bobbed their hair must not wear it bobbed on or off duty." Young ladies with bobbed hair who entered academies, colleges, and nursing schools were permitted to attend upon the condition that they covered their short tresses with "switches."

Two interesting notes of this period are found in Dr. Magan's interoffice correspondence concerning feminine medical students. To the president he wrote: "Indirectly I have understood that Miss —— and Miss —— have bobbed their hair. It is reported to me that Miss —— received permission from Dr. Evans to do this on account of her hair coming out after her illness. I will appreciate it if Dr. Evans will write us a note saying that he advised this, in which case it will make it possible for us to enter Miss —— next month as a cooperative student as usual. We will request, however, that you tell her that she will have to wear a switch when she is on the hospital block, in the cafeteria, or at our church."

The cunning of the feminine mind was discerned by Dr. Percy, as revealed in a note written to the president the following year concerning a young lady—a junior medical student. The dean said: "I talked to Miss —— on Sunday about 3 p.m. relative to the matter of her having bobbed her hair. She tells me she did not know there was anything wrong about it, and that she thought it was perfectly proper even if she did bob it, to go around with switches, etc. I have very good information from others in her class that she boasts that she is going to break the embargo, et cetera. I gave her until Tuesday at 5 o'clock to have her switches on, and have informed her that they must be worn whenever she is on the hospital block or around our premises anywhere, in the cafeteria, at chapel, or at school duties at the County Hospital. She remarked, 'I understand.' I have told her to show herself to Miss Borg and bring me word from Miss Borg that her switches are satisfactory. She told me she did not know when she could get the switches, so I set the time myself, giving her two full weekdays. Since then I understand she has three switches, and does not intend to put them on until the last minute."

No doubt the doctor breathed a sigh of relief on March 23, 1926, when the board voted "to rescind all actions recorded on the minutes with reference to the manner of dressing the hair of women connected with the institution, but that we go on record as favoring the wearing of long hair."

PROBLEMS OF THE C.M.E. STAFF

The dean faced the task of directing a campaign for funds to build the new hospital building. There was also the critical problem of keeping the faculty and hiring new personnel. Because financial stringency haunted some families, a number of the teachers were forced to turn to private medical practice. Dr. Magan realized that the low salaries resulted in an unstable teaching staff. Members of the alumni would have been willing to subsidize some of the faculty, but this would not harmonize with church policy. Yet when some of the teachers faced dire emergencies, the sympathetic dean came to their aid by obtaining private donations to help teachers buy homes or purchase cars when they were "absolutely needed." The doctor sons, Wellesley and Shaen, along with other alumni, contributed to such a fund.

Dr. Magan was strongly opposed to medical doctors in denominational institutions receiving a higher salary than the ministers. When the plan was made to pay medical superintendents of sanitariums a higher wage than other church officials, Dr. Percy said, "If we cannot as medical people work along with the rest of the crowd on the same basis as others, sharing the sacrifices of this cause, we would better get out and go to selling real estate or something else of the sort." When the board raised the salary level of medical-school administrators, the fighting Irish spirit rebelled against accepting the additional money. He expressed his philosophy quite strongly in a letter to the comptroller: "I cannot accept this wage. At the same time I do not want to be decorated with the laurels of either a hero or a martyr for not accepting it. To me there are several quite fundamental reasons and principles involved, something as follows:

"There is a strong sentiment throughout the denomination that our physicians are grasping, and that they look upon themselves as being better or worthy of more money than other ranks among us. I do not believe our doctors mean it this way; many of them have a very hard time and need every penny they get. On the other hand I firmly believe that the more nearly a few of us can set an example by laboring for a wage approximating that of other men in positions of more or less high responsibility among us the better it will be. . . .

"I cannot believe that it is right that as poor a specimen of spirituality as I am should have more wages than the president of the General Conference. I do not believe that I work any harder, if as hard, as you do, and even at my old wage I am getting a great deal more. The same is true of other men. . . . The more nearly we can blend the spirit of the ministry, the physicians, and the businessmen the better it is going to be for all of us. The road may be and is hard at times; however, the less distinction of salary the better. I am sure our doctors will be looked upon with a great deal more favor by our people if we can get them, as times goes on, to put themselves more nearly on the basis of their fellow laborers, and this will be good for the cause which we all dearly love.

"I am not in as hard a place as some of the other men. I do own my home and a little bit besides. I do not want, however, the idea to get abroad that I have plenty of property and money, for this is not the case. . . . Consequently, I will do whichever way you say—either accept a check for $46.50 per week or return you the difference as between that figure and $51 at the end of every month."

And so Dr. Magan returned to the college $4.50 of his salary each week! He was finally persuaded to take the full salary, however, since the treasurer of the General Conference told him he was "creating hard feelings in the minds of others" by his action.

While the zest for life was still strong in Dr. Magan, he faced the issues of the medical school realistically. To his friend, Elder Griggs, he set down this pungent observation: "Running a medical school is a hard job. You have, I think, more elements to deal with in an intimate way than in any other one of our institutions. . . . The ancient mariners were obliged to steer between Scylla and Charybdis. That was bad enough. They had to guide their vessels so as to miss trouble on two sides; we must guide ours so as to miss on three—our ministerial brethren and our folks who are of the church of God, our own Seventh-day Adventist doctors, and the outside men of the American Medical Association and all that goes with it."

15

Taking the Helm

At the session of the board on March 23, 1927, Dr. Evans resigned from the presidency of C.M.E. For some time he had become increasingly interested in pathological research, and the board had given him a leave of absence to join a medical laboratory in Los Angeles. Dr. Risley, of the Loma Linda division, was elected president and Dr. Magan continued as dean. From the correspondence of the time it seems clear that the General Conference leaders were in favor of promoting the dean to the presidency, but there was "local" opposition. Furthermore, Dr. Magan realized he was not always diplomatic, for he said, "I speak my mind too plainly relative to men and things!"

Dr. Percy likened some of the opposition to the Old Testament figure, Shimei, who was skillful at hurling rocks. When this man exhausted his supply of ammunition, he threw dust. "It is much easier," philosophized the doctor, "to dodge a rock than it is dust, although dust is generally an evidence that you haven't got any real rocks to pitch."

The magnanimous Irishman paid tribute to the new head of the school when he wrote: "I do not know of a man I would rather see in the presidency than Dr. Risley as long as Dr. Evans cannot be there, and I will give him my most undivided and heartfelt support. From another angle, I will be very glad when the time comes when I can honorably lay down my burdens here. The place is no easy one, and the only thing that has held me this long is that I do not want to be a coward and run away."

However, the administrative duties soon burdened Dr. Risley and threatened his health. Early in January, 1928, the board informed Dr. Magan that he should plan to take the office of president at the next constituency meeting. When the session convened at Loma Linda on March 18, the dean gave his report, which was well received. That night when Dr. Percy and his friend, Dr. Thomason, retired in one of the cottages on the campus, thoughts of the impending election weighed so heavily upon the dean's mind that he could not sleep. He arose and penned a letter to the chairman of the nominating committee in which he refused to allow his name to be considered.

The next morning Dr. Percy called the chairman of the committee out of its session to hand him the nocturnal letter. It was of no avail, however, for later in the day the veteran administrator was called before the nominating committee and informed that it was unanimous in nominating him for president. Thus, four months after his sixtieth birthday, and after twelve years of service in the medical school, Dr. Magan became president. However, he realized that the stress and strain of administrative duties were wearing him down. Ten days prior to the meeting he had written to his friend, W. T. Knox, former treasurer of the General Conference, now a member of the C.M.E. board: "I am now well past my sixtieth anniversary, and I am beginning to feel tired and worn from the constant strain and stress of endeavoring to administer, compose, and discipline student affairs. I love to work with our medical students, but I am sure you will recognize that they are in many ways a harder group to handle than the younger class of pupil we get in our literary schools. This is especially true of those in the junior and senior year here. They are soon to be out for themselves, engaged in a profession which will bring them a splendid position and ample means.

"I am weary of it all, and now I am asking that you will do me the favor of using your influence to have me released from this type of work forevermore. I want to get into something either in the school or out of it that will not have so many perplexing and worrying details in it as the work which I have done in Los Angeles for the last eleven years has brought to me. I will be glad to take work of a more general nature—raising money, talking to the students, and endeavoring to shape their characters, getting men to foreign fields, et cetera—if that is the desire of my brethren, but I do ask to be relieved at this coming meeting from the position I have held so long, and I ask this without any reference or proviso as to the matter of title."

THE LOS ANGELES COUNTY HOSPITAL

The astute mind and statesmanlike nature of the veteran educator were sorely needed at this time, both for the school and for another institution in the vicinity. The Los Angeles County Hospital, of which Dr. Magan was a board member, was in a serious situation. Its status was of vital importance to C.M.E., since it was linked to the hospital for much of the teaching of clinical medicine and surgery. Then, too, the standing of interns in the hospital was jeopardized by the conflict.

The problem originated in 1922 when the osteopaths and chiropractors, by a state initiative victory, were given the right to have their own board of examiners and other privileges. The osteopaths petitioned the board of supervisors of the Los Angeles County Hospital to grant them representation on the hospital staff along with doctors with M.D. degrees. This request was granted, and a committee of three M.D.'s and three osteopaths formulated a workable plan. A building with 140 beds, operating rooms, and accommodations for interns and residents was designated as the osteopathic hospital.

However, in 1925, the American College of Surgeons opposed this arrangement, and Dr. Magan was selected to represent the hospital in Chicago at a meeting of medical officials. When the situation was explained fully, Dr. M. T. MacEachern, associate director of the American College of Surgeons, agreed to the arrangement as long as the units were separate and distinct. By 1928, however, a few months after Dr. Magan became president of C.M.E., the Los Angeles County Hospital was notified by the American College of Surgeons that it would be "obliged to remove" the hospital "from approved list of hospitals as it now embraces an osteopathic unit under its administration." Dr. Neal N. Wood, medical director of the hospital, appealed the verdict, and the American College of Surgeons agreed to keep the institution on the approved list until January 1, 1929. The chief points at issue centered around certain procedures: the consultations between osteopaths and M.D.'s, the transfer of patients, case histories, and various administrative details. The medical director was helpless to change these procedures since he was carrying out the action of the board of supervisors. Dr. MacEachern argued that if the Los Angeles County Hospital were allowed to continue on this plan, the nationwide fight against irregular practitioners would be lost.

In friendly and diplomatic language, flavored with the Bible, Dr. Magan addressed a letter to Dr. MacEachern: "All through this struggle I have sought wisdom from a higher Source," he said, "and have trusted that I might be imbued with the word of one of old, 'Let every man be swift to hear, slow to speak, slow to wrath: for the wrath of man worketh not the righteousness of God.' Somehow or other I cannot feel that arguing gets any of us very far at any time or in any place, and I often think of what Lord Avebury, I believe erstwhile Lord Chief Justice of England, once wrote: 'For success in life, tact is more important than talent. . . . Argument is always a little dangerous. It often leads to coolness and misunderstandings. You may gain your argument but lose your friend, which is probably a bad bargain.' After all, kindliness, gentleness, and willingness to see the other man's problem are superresistance in the very best sense."

Dr. Magan reviewed the history of the problem, and how Dr. MacEachern had previously approved of the arrangement. Then he continued: "From that day down to the hour when a few weeks ago Dr. N. N. Wood received your letter stating that the Los Angeles County General Hospital would be stricken from the roll of hospitals called standard by the American College of Surgeons, there was never the shade of a shadow of a doubt that crossed my mind in this subject. I was clear and settled and certain in my own mind upon it as I am that I breathe at the present moment. And, my dear man, with the fullest respect for every statement you have made regarding the matter, and fully according to you the same degree of fairness and squareness in your memory of this transaction as I am sure you will accord me, I cannot recall to my mind any statement being made at our conference which would involve a request on your part, or an agreement on mine, for complete administrative autonomy for the osteopathic division of the hospital, for if such a thing could have been obtained from the board of supervisors there would never have been any need for our conference at all."

Finally, referring to the struggle which physicians in southern California had made to preserve a high standard of medicine, the president of C.M.E. said: "A vastly large majority of our men in southern California feel that we here have borne the brunt of the fight; . . . that we have spent freely of our time and treasure and life in the battle; . . . that during all the years that we have been engaged in this struggle we have never been offered any assistance, neither men or money, by the great medical organizations of our country, your own included. If now, after we have struggled and done our best, you, as in a general way I set forth at our conference in Chicago in 1925, shall embarrass us by blacklisting Unit No. 1 of the Los Angeles County General Hospital, it will be impossible for us to feel otherwise to our dying day than that our own professional brethren have turned upon us and stabbed us to the heart."

In spite of this straightforward appeal, on January 2, 1929, Dr. Franklin Martin, Director of the American College of Surgeons, restated the verdict against the county hospital. However, he said the College of Surgeons would "postpone the publishing of the announcement of our list of approved hospitals for three months."

OIL ON TROUBLED WATERS

The county hospital administration next requested Dr. Magan and Dr. William Cutter, dean of the University of Southern California Medical School, to seek the support of Dr. Wilbur, president of Stanford University, who had recently been appointed Secretary of Commerce in the Hoover Cabinet. On February 1 the men counseled with Dr. Wilbur on the Palo Alto campus. He was most cordial, and agreed to support the Los Angeles County Hospital case before the American College of Surgeons. He was at a loss to understand how this august body would break its agreement. At that point Dr. Percy remarked, "The Good Book states that 'he that sweareth to his own hurt and changeth not' shall stand in Mount Zion."

"I don't know anything about Mount Zion," replied the Stanford University president, "but I know he would stand better with me!"

On October 14, 1929, despite the efforts of Dr. Magan and other influential physicians, the American College of Surgeons, at its annual session, passed out a hospital standardization report which omitted the Los Angeles County Hospital from the list of approved institutions. However, the Council on Medical Education stood by the hospital and Dr. Colwell declared that this organization would continue to maintain its rating. The Council would also issue a special bulletin to the deans of all colleges stating that the county hospital was approved for interns and that its status had in no way been impaired because of the liaison with the osteopaths.

In an optimistic mood, Dr. Magan reported the happenings of the Chicago session to Dr. Wood: "Now all with whom I have talked so far feel that the thing for us to do is to lie low. . . . We will get all the interns we want, and we have a host of friends who will help us get them. In the end, I am satisfied that the whole thing will be like the nice moral taught in the Ingoldsby's Legends about the Jackdaw of Rheims. Did you ever read it? The cardinal of Rheims lost his cardinal's ring. He caused search to be everywhere made but to no avail. Then he pronounced a solemn curse upon the thief. The whole thing is in poetry, and I cannot just now remember the rhyme. The substance, however, is that the cardinal cursed him in eating and drinking and sleeping, he cursed him in walking and thinking and talking; he cursed him with bell and he cursed him with book; he cursed him with candle, might he dream of the devil and wake in a fright:—*'but what gave rise to no little surprise was that nobody* *seemed one penny the worse!** . . . the less we have to say the sooner the thing will die down."

However, the animosity of certain medical men in the national organization continued to focus on the expanding Los Angeles County Hospital and its personnel; but the institution, guided by a sound, strategic policy, weathered the storm. The American Medical Association finally settled the issues peaceably and the hospital prospered. Again, the close-knit friendships and the sound judgment of Dr. Percy helped the two medical institutions in the Los Angeles area—both the county hospital and C.M.E.

THE PERIPATETIC PRESIDENT

Problems! There was a never-ending stream of them, with the medical school on two campuses. On one occasion President Magan declared, "This whole matter of a divided institution is a very expensive one." Many of the serious items came in pairs—two faculties, two hospitals, two nurses' training schools, two sets of buildings. During the late twenties the fad for surveys, reports, and questionnaires was developing in medical as well as other educational circles. Dr. Magan complained of the trend, and said he longed for the day when certain officials would not be "butting in all the time," a hope that many other educators were to express in the next three decades! The questionnaires and requests for reports from societies and organizations were "almost beyond count."

Issues of the A.M.A. and the California State Medical Association occupied days of the president's time, but the results were beneficial

---

*The doctor was remembering a stanza of Richard Barham's poem, "The Jackdaw of Rheims," which is as follows:

"The Cardinal rose with a dignified look,
He called for his candle, his bell, and his book:
In holy anger, and pious grief
He solemnly cursed that rascally thief!
He cursed him at board, he cursed him in bed,
From the sole of his foot to the crown of his head!
He cursed him in sleeping, that every night
He should dream of the devil, and wake in a fright;
He cursed him in eating, he cursed him in drinking,
He cursed him in coughing, in sneezing, in winking;
He cursed him in sitting, in standing, in lying;
He cursed him in walking, in riding, in flying;
He cursed him in living, he cursed him in dying!
Never was heard such a terrible curse!
But what gave rise
To no little surprise,
Nobody seemed one penny the worse!"

to C.M.E. For example, while Dr. Magan was in Chicago in 1929, attending a session of the Council of Medical Education, he was able to reconcile the differences between the National Board of Medical Examiners and the California Board of Medical Examiners. This reconciliation paved the way for a legislative act which permitted doctors holding National Board certificates to register in the State of California, a "great assistance to us [C.M.E. graduates]."

Dr. Percy drove himself constantly, with long hours in the office, and endless days on the road attending councils and medical-association conclaves, as well as visiting alumni and donors of the school. The pace was telling, however, and while in Detroit in October, 1929, after a strenuous Eastern trip, the peripatetic doctor noted for the first time in his diary that his heart "was making a fool of itself."

DAYS OF DEPRESSION

Financial difficulties increased as the depression struck the American economy. Since the shock was felt around the world, the General Conference proposed a slash in the medical college budget, with the workers taking a salary cut of from 5 to 20 percent. Dr. Magan, a veteran of austerity, faced the crisis realistically. He reasoned that the church organization could not do more to subsidize the school, and "it is up to us to make the thing go or turn it over to someone who can." He was certain the staff of the medical institutions at Loma Linda and Los Angeles would be willing to accept the reduction of wages when they saw the seriousness of the emergency. The college must, said the president, "get down to bedrock and put things on a better basis." It was a day to "eliminate extravagance and waste" and to "make personal sacrifices."

For several years Dr. Percy had dreamed of retracing his round-the-world trip of the nineties; and the board voted such an itinerary for him so that he might go to Europe, India, and the Far East, visiting medical institutions and encouraging alumni in foreign service. Because of the financial stringency, however, Dr. Magan requested that the action be rescinded, and his dreams were never fulfilled.

As the clouds of the depression grew darker, the hospitals on the two campuses felt the stringency. By October, 1932, the White Memorial Hospital was down to fifty patients. When the sick of the distressed areas of Los Angeles could not afford hospital care, the college organized a group of nurses—known as the Ellen White nurses—who went to work among "the very poorest and most starved classes in the city." The women donated their time to the project, the hospital gave them their board, and the county paid their carfare.

The depression days gave some compensation, at least, to a veteran traveler, who had known how independent the railroads could be in their treatment of passengers. In 1931 the railroads were seeking business, and "they can't be too polite to you," Dr. Percy observed. The information desk oozed with sweetness when the clerk said, "I will be most delighted to secure your reservations for you; and I trust you will have a pleasant trip." After purchasing a ticket in the Chicago office, the doctor inquired as to the whereabouts of a public telephone. The agent, wreathed in smiles, thrust the office phone into his hands, urging him to use it as long as he desired. Philosophically Magan observed, "Surely and verily the depression yieldeth the peaceable fruits of accommodation and politeness!"

AN HONORED PRESIDENT

As the result of his years of friendship with medical-association officers Dr. Magan was elected to board positions and honored with important speaking appointments. In 1932 he was appointed a member of the California State Board of Medical Examiners, and the junior class congratulated him on his "untiring efforts" to bring "honor and prestige" to the institution.

A year earlier the Irishman delivered an unusual address, "The Role of the Medical School in the Development of Character in Medical Students," before the Association of American Medical Colleges at its New Orleans session. The importance of this message, filled with numerous Biblical allusions, weighed heavily upon the man even before he arrived in the Southern city. In describing the incident, he said, "In the train going down to New Orleans the last night before we got in, and I was to present the paper in the morning, I could not sleep; I lay awake practically all night long. I prayed and prayed and prayed that God would help me that something might be accomplished, and about half past four or five a great peace filled my soul and it seemed to me that an angel of God had come into my berth. I felt clear then that God was going to work. The Lord certainly laid hold upon the hearts of those men. So many of them came to me afterwards. Dr. Louis B. Wilson, Director of the Mayo Foundation at Rochester, Minnesota, came and said, 'Magan, your paper has settled me. I must work for the souls of the students in the future and not so much for the scientific side of things.' Dr. Stanley Ryerson, of the Medical Department of the University of Toronto, who is a really great man and had charge of the Canadian Medical Forces or at least a large part of them during the war, grasped my hands with the word, 'Dr. Magan, that sounded as if Dr. Osler had risen from the dead; that is what we need.' Several of the men came to me and asked me where the texts were and wanted me to write down the references for them."

But age crept on inexorably, and Dr. Percy saw some of his colleagues dropping by the way. By 1932, Dr. Musgrave had died; Dr. Colwell had been forced to resign his important post with the Council of Medical Education because of a cerebral hemorrhage; and Dr. Morris Fishbein had been incapacitated as the result of an auto accident.

Dr. Percy had several sieges of illness which kept him from councils and medical association meetings. Disappointed because he could not attend the 1932 Autumn Council in Battle Creek, he wrote his board associates who were at the session: "The folks here seemed quite worried in regard to my going but knowing my determination said but little. When, however, your wire came, everyone seemed to feel very clear that we should accept your counsel and that I should remain."

But the fighting spirit of the man was undaunted by his infirmities. With a chuckle he could tell Dr. Sutherland, "Please do not worry about my health. I am working from early morning till late at night; and while I am not as well as I was five or ten years ago, I think I can get just as much or more done in a day's work than any three of the rest of them put together, at least I pride myself on this and it comforts me whether it is true or not."

And in the midst of the heated controversy over the Los Angeles County Hospital, when the physician was doing all he could to protect the interests of that institution as well as those of C.M.E., someone accused him of being the "smartest political doctor in southern California." When he heard the remark, he said, "Cheerio. There is nothing like having people think you amount to something, even if you don't!"

16

The Vision Undimmed by Shadows

The Magans enjoyed their children and grandchildren, and they believed in "togetherness." The president once said of his sons, "Wellesley and Shaen are the joy of our lives, and we have great times with both of them, and now Val is almost twenty-one." The doctor sons keenly felt the depression in their Covina medical practice, where they found collections difficult and "heart-rending." To get away from their heavy burdens, Drs. Wellesley and Shaen alternated their summer vacations. They would hitch a trailer to a car, and, with complete camping equipment and an outboard motor stowed away, head for the mountains and lakes. In 1932 Shaen's family journeyed to Canada; and after they returned, Wellesley and his family vacationed in Yellowstone National Park.

The next year in August, Shaen and Marie, and their seven-year-old son, Robert, with their trailer and camping equipment in tow, drove to Yellowstone. Accompanying them was George Steckles, a young man who had worked for the physicians, and who took the wheel on several long trips to relieve Shaen. When the vacationers arrived in the park, they made their camp not far from Yellowstone Lake. The glorious days of rest and relaxation passed all too rapidly, and on Thursday morning, August 31, the Magans decided to break camp that afternoon and leave the park before nightfall. During the early morning hours, however, the four campers fished in the lake from an eighteen-foot steel rowboat powered with an outboard motor. Because of choppy water the fishing was poor. Shortly after nine o'clock Shaen headed the boat for the shore, and Marie got out and went to the camp to prepare breakfast. With half a gallon of gasoline left in the tank of the outboard motor, the men decided to take one more short cruise on the lake.

Marie prepared breakfast and waited expectantly for the hungry men; but they never came. When she reported their absence, the park rangers organized searching parties to scour the lake for a trace of the boat. A mountain storm had broken in sudden but intense fury, and the craft was believed to have been swamped by the waves.

In the afternoon, when no trace of the trio had been found, Marie called Dr. Wellesley and told him of her fears. The son relayed the disconcerting news to the San Marino home, and soon Dr. Percy and his wife were on the highway to Covina. At ten o'clock that night, one of the Magan cars, with five close friends of the family, left for Yellowstone. Through the dark hours Dr. Percy, his wife, and the Wellesley Magans maintained an agonizing vigil at the Covina home, awaiting a telephone message.

Not until forty-eight hours later, however, did searchers find the boat, its stern on the floor of the lake in sixteen feet of water and the bow barely hidden by the waves. Dr. Shaen's body was found some thirty feet from the boat, with Bobby close by. The body of George Steckles was a little distance away. Dr. Percy recounted the theory of the park rangers and old-timers as to how the tragedy must have occurred. When the storm struck, the lake was churned by the gale, and the men in the craft decided to turn and head for the shore. But before the motor could get the boat under way a wave must have dashed over the stern, swamping the craft and sinking it immediately. "Naturally enough," said Dr. Percy, "little Bobby would have been frightened, and Shaen and George immediately made for him. I suppose that he was difficult to handle and control and that, with the weight of their heavy clothes, sweaters, and boots, made it almost impossible to do anything. The fact that Shaen, wonderful swimmer that he was, was within only thirty feet of the boat, would tend to show that he had stuck to Bobby, and had never been really able to get under way to start for the shore. George Steckles probably did likewise until Bobby and Shaen went down, and then he struck out; but he was so exhausted he only lasted a few feet farther."

The funeral service was held in the Covina Methodist Church on Sabbath afternoon, September 9, with the family friend, Dr. Thomason, reading the life sketch. The city of Covina closed its stores and shops in honor of the physician whose loss they mourned, and over two thousand persons passed the caskets where lay the bodies of the doctor and his young son. Dr. Percy confessed to the brother that this was "the hardest day I think I have ever been called upon to pass through in my old life." But faith in God's overruling providence sustained him in the hour of test. "I do not feel bitter," he wrote. "I feel very grateful to God for all His goodness and loving-kindness to us through all our lives long. And we can only say with Job of old, 'The Lord gave, and the Lord hath taken away; blessed be the name of the Lord.' "

"GUARD WELL OUR PATH"

Another inspection of the medical college—the most "thorough and exhaustive" yet conducted—was scheduled for sometime between 1934 and 1935. The Association of American Medical Colleges, the Council on Medical Education and Hospitals of the A.M.A., and the State Boards of Medical Examiners had joined in a far-reaching survey of every medical school in the nation. In describing the proposed inspection, the president of C.M.E. told the General Conference officers: "It is described as being 'the most momentous undertaking' of its kind which has ever been launched—'no similar piece of work has ever been done and expectations run high and wide as to what it will accomplish.' There can be no question but what the medical powers that be have big things in their heads. They have openly announced that there is a large difference today between the best medical colleges and the poorest in our land, as there was in the early years of this century when they cut the number of medical schools almost exactly in half, putting 50 percent of these institutions out of business. These men are firmly of the opinion that some medical schools will have to go. I do not think they have us particularly in mind, possibly not at all in mind; I cannot say, for I do not know. However, I do realize that when it comes to buildings and equipment and to the size of teaching personnel that we are almost hopelessly behind practically every other medical college in the land. Of course, if they see that we are doing things to improve our building and equipment items, they will be much more inclined to do leniency with us than otherwise."

With careful strategy Dr. Magan used the imminent inspection as a lever to pry more funds from the board for much-needed buildings and equipment. At the 1934 Autumn Council of the General Conference he was able to get appropriations of half a million dollars to put the school in shape for the inspection committee. He was actually not worried about the rating of the school, for he knew his friends in medical education circles would stand by the institution. There was Dr. Zapffe, a sincere admirer of C.M.E., who had given counsel and assistance in hours of difficulty. Dr. William Cutter, secretary of the Council on Medical Education and Hospitals, had succeeded Dr. Colwell; indeed, Dr. Percy had been "instrumental in getting him his job." There was also Dr. Olin West, executive secretary of the American Medical Association, who had been a close friend since Percy attended medical school. These fraternal ties were a strength to C.M.E. in days of uncertainty, and the administrator could say, "I . . . have done everything in my power to guard well our path and guide well our ship."

"UNLOOKED-FOR TROUBLES"

Before the inspectors visited the school, however, perplexing issues faced the administration. The year 1935 could be termed a period of "one terrific battle after another with all sorts of perplexities and unlooked-for troubles, mostly within ourselves."

There were pressures from the Harveian Society of the alumni for a large-scale program of research, and representation of the graduates on the board of trustees. Criticism of the organization of certain departments, changes in faculty personnel, and financial crises cast shadows over the campus. Then, too, some of the alumni were discontented over the building program and because they could not practice surgery in the hospital. (The rules of the Council on Medical Education and Hospitals did not allow teaching hospitals to be open to any physicians except members of the teaching faculty.)

When a group of the alumni met in Battle Creek early in 1936, Dr. Percy sent a message of conciliation through Dr. G. Mosser Taylor. "I will appreciate it," said the president, "if you will tell the men that the dearest thing to me in all the earth is the welfare of the College of Medical Evangelists and its graduates. I love every one of the men who have passed through the portals of this school as if he were my own kin and flesh and blood. . . . I long and pray above all other things to see a deep and moving spiritual life lay hold of each individual of our faculty, each student in the school, and each and every alumnus in the wide field at home and over the rolling seas. . . . I trust that as long as God shall give me breath and strength that I may humbly and in the fear of God labor for all that is in me to better the school scientifically and materially. My own knowledge of medical science, as you know, is far from being great, therefore, I am convinced that my role will be to help the rest of you good men who are giving your lives to this school to obtain wisdom and good training."

There was also a reaction in the field to the accreditation program of the colleges, and at the 1935 Autumn Council, Dr. Percy reported that "a wave" swept over the assembly "against accrediting." Only two institutions—Pacific Union College and Emmanuel Missionary College—were permitted to be accredited. Again the medical-school rating was in jeopardy, and the president of C.M.E. pleaded with the leaders to have "good judgment" and "a sound mind."

The inspection committee, Dr. Herman Weiskotten and Surgeon General M. W. Ireland, arrived in Los Angeles on March 8, 1936, and immediately notified Dr. Magan that they would like to visit with him at the Biltmore Hotel. For four hours they fired questions at him "with all the speed and precision and accuracy of machine-gun fire." After the interview, the Irishman said with a smile, he felt like asking the Lord to do to Drs. Weiskotten and Ireland what He said He would do to the prophet Ezekiel, namely, "And I will make thy tongue cleave to the roof of thy mouth, that thou shalt be dumb."

A SYMPATHETIC EXAMINING COMMITTEE

The examiners were most considerate, however, when they visited the two campuses, and the religious atmosphere left its impress. When a small group of physicians sat down to eat in the Loma Linda Sanitarium dining room, Dr. Magan asked Dr. Risley to say grace. Impressed by this prayer, Dr. Weiskotten said, "This is the first meal to which I have sat down since I left home where the blessing was asked. It sounded good to me. In our home Mrs. Weiskotten and myself and the children always have Bible reading and prayer in the morning, and we say grace before every meal."

When the visitors questioned the president as to why there should be "a College of Medical Evangelists," he presented them with a bound document of fifty mimeographed pages which set forth the plan of the school, the endowment note program, the distribution of the alumni, and the aims of Seventh-day Adventists in sponsoring a balanced health message. The examiners were pleased to find that 31 percent of C.M.E. graduates were employed by the church in the homeland and in foreign countries. They were interested, too, in the spirit of sacrifice which permeated the alumni who went to India, Africa, or China, as well as the faculty of the medical college.

There were deserved criticisms of teaching methods and of the shortage of personnel in certain departments; but, on the whole, the school made a deep, positive impression. Driving back to the hotel on the last day of inspection, Dr. Ireland said, "Well, I'm hypnotized by that place." And when the men got out of the car, they declared, "This has been the greatest day since we started out on this work. We have enjoyed every minute of it!"

Before the men left, they dispelled any fears that the president might have concerning the standing of C.M.E. "We think you have a most wonderful school," said Dr. Weiskotten, "capable of splendid development, and you are in no danger whatsoever of being taken off the accredited list or put on probation. Some suggestions, of course, will be made, but you are a splendid school, and we are as proud of you as of any school we have visited."

In spite of all the preparations that had been made for the inspection committee and the optimism of President Magan, the medical school was placed on probation in the autumn of 1936. This was a confidential report, said Dr. Cutter, and no publication of the status would be made. He added: "When you feel that the deficiencies noted by the Council have been corrected and that the school is meeting in a satisfactory manner the prevailing standards, application may be made to the Council for reconsideration with a view to restoring the school to a position of unqualified approval."

In addition to this blow, Dr. Zapffe had written a month earlier concerning the scholarship of the students. When he examined the annual report of C.M.E., he found that of the 102 freshmen, "only 42 percent came through with a clear record; 53 percent had conditions and failures or withdrew failing or failed." The secretary of the Association of American Medical Colleges then asked, "Isn't that rather startling? When I see that state of affairs I wonder whether the students are not well selected, whether they are not the right sort, whether the teaching is not good, or whether the teachers are hard or, perhaps, poor examiners. Surely, something is not as it should be, and it would be well to sort of 'take stock.' "

ILLNESS STRIKES AGAIN

Whether all of this disappointing information affected Dr. Percy's physical condition is not known. However, within a week after Dr. Cutter's letter arrived, the Irishman took to his bed with such excruciating pain in his left leg that he was forced to lie on his right side most of the time. He described his malady as neuritis involving the lumbosacral plexus of nerves. Even in the throes of the painful illness which kept him bedfast for months, he did not lose his sense of humor. To Dr. Cutter he could write: "I am progressing slowly, but I am making progress. . . . I might be lots worse than I am. I have no fever, my pain is gradually disappearing. I am having a tough time with my appetite now, and they are feeding me concentrated cod-liver oil—phew—kas—bas—and other abominable-tasting stuff, but when a fellow is down and can't get up, he has to take what they hand him. When your leg is tied up the way mine is, you simply can't get away. I think I feel somewhat like my nurse told me about herself when she was expecting confinement and it came right down to the first pains. She said she would have given all the world then if she could have backed out of it all, but there was no way on the face of the earth to do it. That is about the way with me, and I would like to get out of this, but I can't."

In April, 1937, the constituency passed a resolution of appreciation and sympathy to C.M.E.'s president in his prolonged illness, and the faculty of the Los Angeles division sent him a letter rich with devotion and understanding. In part it read: "Dear Dr. Percy, our hearts have yearned for you during these long months of your forced confinement; our prayers have daily been burdened with your name. Your face is sadly missed in all our gatherings. In the very many perplexing problems which in your absence we try to solve, we find ourselves greatly needing your wise words of counsel. . . . Dear colleague, in the long, weary, and lonesome hours of your waiting for returning strength, please be assured of our deepest devotion, our loyal cooperation, and our most solicitous prayers for your complete restoration to health and in God's own providential time, your return to our midst and to your unsupplied place as our wise, consecrated counselor and guide."

THREESCORE AND TEN YEARS

The months of illness caused Dr. Percy to realize that he could no longer continue to shoulder the heavy administrative burdens of the school. He reminded Elder J. L. McElhany, president of the General Conference, of a conference they had had on the subject, and that the board must "be looking around to find someone to put in training to take my place as I could not expect to continue carrying the load that I have been carrying."

The areas of administration were studied by the board of trustees, and at the October 28 session they voted to call Dr. George T. Harding III to connect with the college as assistant to the president.

The seventieth birthday of Percy Magan fell on Sabbath, November 13, 1937. The next afternoon a birthday celebration was given by Dr. Wellesley and his wife at their Covina home, with more than two hundred guests present to wish the physician Godspeed and many more years of happiness.

Dr. Percy believed that men who had the vision of the work to be accomplished were often very much alone in their thinking. To Dr. Harding, who was considering the invitation to help build a stronger medical school, the aging president wrote: "Your situation in this respect is something the same as that of Daniel when he wrote, 'And I Daniel *alone* saw the vision; for the men that were with me saw not the vision; but a great quaking fell upon them, so that they fled to hide themselves.' It is ever thus. The man that sees the vision must go ahead and do the things which need to be done. Those who don't see are subject 'to a great quaking'; in other words, they feel that everything will go to rack and ruin because of what you have done. I have known this to work out in my life many, many times. . . . I so often think of that which is written in Isaiah's great prophecy: 'Look unto Abraham your father, and unto Sarah that bare you: for I called him *alone,* and blessed him, and increased him.'

'Now, the point I want to make, George, is this—God through all the ages never seemed to get a group of men in His mind, cull them over, and finally pick one of them to do a certain piece of work. As Bible scenes pass before me, I cannot recall such an incident anywhere. The eternal Word stands, 'I CALLED HIM ALONE.' In other words, God fastens His mind on one man and on that man *alone* for a certain piece of work, and He calls that man just as long as there is any hope in all the world that that man will accept the call."

17

A Fighter to the End

When the Council on Medical Education recommended that the enrollment of the freshman class in medicine be limited to fifty-five or sixty students, the Adventist Church was confronted with a difficult situation. How should it meet the demands of its youth for a professional education? In 1938 the administration of the medical school made the initial step toward transforming the institution into a university. At that time Dr. Magan envisioned a school of dentistry in connection with C.M.E. He wrote to Dr. Cutter for an opinion on such a plan, and the secretary of the Council on Medical Education replied: "There are a good many universities in which dental and medical students receive their training in the basic medical sciences in the same departments of anatomy, chemistry, physiology, et cetera; but almost without exception they are taught in separate classes. The obvious reason for this is that medical students in general are better qualified than dental students; and if the classes are combined, the level of instruction must either be too low for the medical group or too high for the dental group. If dental and medical students are taught separately, there must be a larger departmental staff. It is, of course, quite reasonable to use the same laboratories at different hours, or preferably at different periods of the year."

Thus the groundwork for a broader program of training was laid by the far-seeing educator; and although the dream never came true in his lifetime, he would have rejoiced to see the founding of Loma Linda University, with its various professional schools, including dentistry.

At this time two recommendations came to the school from medical-education officials: first, the entrance requirements should be raised; and second, full-time teachers with adequate specialized training should be hired for various departments. Furthermore, the faculty was commended for its "scientific contributions," and Dr. Percy was praised for his efforts to bring a "higher level" of scholarship and scientific research to the school.

When Dr. Harding did not accept the invitation of the board to join the administration of the school, Dr. Percy continued the search for an "assistant to the president." To Dr. T. R. Flaiz, who was being considered for the position, the Irishman gave this counsel: "You will realize I am getting along in years. I will be seventy-one next November, and I cannot expect to be active in a forceful way for many more years if it should please God that time should last for a season and a time. . . . It has generally been considered that my line of duty should be in conferences with the deans relative to their problems, in matters connected with the American Medical Association and the General Conference, large affairs of the National Board of Medical Examiners, and with the Association of American Medical Colleges."

Dr. Magan's program, still a busy one, did not prevent him from attending medical meetings or keep him from speaking appointments. After addressing the Public Health League, he noted in his diary: "There were about two hundred people present. They seemed interested; no one died or went to sleep."

RAISING MEDICAL-EDUCATION STANDARDS

In 1939 the medical school faced another inspection by the American Medical Association and the Association of American Medical Colleges. Persistent pressure was being exerted to force the school to increase its facilities for research and to expand the graduate training program of the faculty. After the visit of the inspection committee in April, Dr. Weiskotten made several constructive criticisms. He wrote:

"1. The school is a divided school. Such an organization always presents serious handicaps, and these handicaps are increasing with the present trends in medical education. Both preclinical and clinical departments suffer from geographic separation.

"2. The maintenance of adequate library facilities for both divisions of a divided school also presents difficulties. . . . It appears necessary to continue the College of Medical Evangelists as a divided school, at least for the immediate future, and it is recognized that this school does have a sanatorium available at the Loma Linda Division. However, it is important to recognize the handicaps in connection with such an organization. . . .

"It is recommended that the curriculum be so planned as to permit the transfer of students from the Loma Linda Division to the Los Angeles Division of the school not later than the middle of the second year."

It is interesting to note that the recommendation to transfer a portion of the students to the Los Angeles Division "not later than the middle of the second year" was voted twenty-two years later!

The aging administrator felt the tremendous pressure of rising medical standards. "Things are getting harder and harder," he opined, "and there is no question in my mind but what we are being obliged to do things under very difficult circumstances that might have been [done] years ago under very easy circumstances."

By 1940 the heart of the valiant fighter was showing the strain of battle, and he was forced to remain in bed for weeks at a stretch. One day, after an attack, Dr. Percy sat in the patio of his San Marino home and wrote: "The doctors are still keeping me quite quiet on account of my heart, and it takes but little to upset it. However, both Dr. Clarke and Dr. William Leake, whom he brought in as a consultant, and who, by the way, was an old classmate of mine in Vanderbilt University, Tennessee, feel that I am making a fine recovery except that they always qualify by saying, 'It is slow and at your age will be slow.' I feel very, very grateful to God for His loving-kindness and the multitude of His tender mercies toward me, but I do long and long and long, Brother McElhany, to be able to do a great big day's work again! . . . I have spent some fifty-four years in this work—more than half a century. Whether I am to be privileged to see the great Master come, I do not know."

When World War II exploded over Europe in September, 1939, the doctor was deeply depressed. Soon he received news that two of his nephews were in the British army; that Sheelah, his brother's eldest daughter, was chief dietitian in a British naval hospital; and that dangers beset his homeland on every side. To his friend Mrs. Tracy he wrote: "This terrible affair in Europe which sooner or later is bound to reach us and involve us has cast a deep gloom and an unspeakable sorrow over all of us."

Because of plans made twenty years earlier, at the close of World War I, the medical school was able to organize and sponsor the 47th General Hospital for the Army. In defense of this measure Dr. Magan wrote the President of the General Conference: "First of all, it must be borne in mind that we had this hospital at the time of World War I. It was never called out, because the war came to an end; but the College of Medical Evangelists and especially the White Memorial Hospital sponsored it by request of the Government. . . . When the war closed the hospital only lived in skeleton form. . . .

"Only recently, but before this move for the draft was initiated, a number of our doctors in the medical reserve corps were called to the Presidio for special training. . . . All through the years we have kept the 47th General Hospital alive and have because of this gained high favor with the Army, the Ninth Corps Area Commander, the Surgeon General, and even the Secretary of War. . . .

"The difficulties which confronted us for a while lay in the fact that everything in regard to the draft and in regard to the medical corps and its organization was being rushed so that the Army machine was not working smoothly. . . .

"The 47th General Hospital personnel is made up of picked men who have a knowledge of what has to be done in an Army general hospital and who have had some training for the same. . . . It is a fundamental principle of military hospital organization to endeavor to secure just as far as humanly possible men who know each other and who have worked together. . . . The 47th General Hospital is composed of twenty-eight medical officers; one chaplain; one quartermaster; six medical administrative officers; two from the regular Army—one being a commanding officer and the other an executive officer. The idea is that the regular Army fellows will step out as soon as our men are entirely initiated. There is a total enlisted personnel of 400, and 120 women nurses."

June, 1942, at the close of the school year, was the date fixed by Dr. Percy for him to turn the helm of the medical college over to Dr. W. E. Macpherson. In the previous March, the Irishman had notified the Los Angeles County Medical Advisory Board that he would be stepping out of his board position—which he had held since January, 1917. To honor Dr. Percy, the Board elected him a member emeritus of both the staff and the Advisory Board.

On May 13, the junior and senior medical classes sponsored a farewell party for the retiring president. One of the speakers for the occasion was Dr. George H. Kress, who had known Dr. Percy from the time he arrived in Los Angeles to be the dean of C.M.E., and had worked with him on the board of the Los Angeles County Hospital. In his tribute Dr. Kress said, "In all the years it has been my privilege to work with Percy Magan, he always kept troth; and I never have had occasion to doubt his faith and loyal support, once he committed himself as being in favor of a principle at stake, or an objective to which we were committed. . . . Percy Tilson Magan was born, and has been at all times, intrinsically and always a gentleman; . . . his life course has been so run that he has proved an inspiration to the younger disciples of the profession of the healing art."

When he retired from administrative duties, the doctor was urged by the board, as he had been before, to write the history of the medical work of the denomination. However, he was not ready to think only of history; he was still ready to *make* it, for he took a dynamic stand at many a board session. After one stormy meeting he wrote, "I fear I was pretty wrathy, and I think a number of them [board members] did not like it very well. But if there is one thing that annoys me above another it is when people will not stand up for their friends but are too fearful of their own hides." On another occasion he described his reactions in this manner: "Board meeting, and we had a pretty warm time of it. Scrapped a lot, and I felt better after the scrap than before it!"

When he did pause to look back over the years, he made the poignant observation that "practically every one of the men and women of note who had anything to do with the starting of the school was dead and gone—Ellen G. White, W. C. White, John Burden, A. G. Daniells, and George Irwin." As president emeritus, the doctor continued for some months to preach in the churches, visit the two campuses, and enjoy contacts with a host of friends and relatives. Gradually, however, he tapered off his work. Soon illness confined him to his home, and his days of public ministry were ended. On December 16, 1947, he died of a heart attack. The private funeral was held on Friday, December 19, and a memorial service was conducted in Paulson Hall, Sabbath afternoon, December 20.

Some of the doctor's intimate friends were on the platform for this memorial hour, Elder Griggs and Drs. Macpherson, Wirth, D. D. Comstock, and William F. Norwood. One of Dr. Percy's favorite songs, "Sunset and Evening Star," was sung by Dr. Robert L. Marsh. Dr. Wirth well summarized the contributions of the man when he said, "He was eminent as a student, a teacher, an administrator, as a speaker, as a preacher of the Word of God. . . . What a work he did in education, in the great South, and above all, for this institution—the College of Medical Evangelists!"

18

He Was Gifted in Communication

To listen to one of his lectures or sermons, to read an article from his pen, was to discover Dr. Magan's varied interests and his wide range of reading. Beginning with teen-age explorations in the library of the retired banker, Levi Moore, in Red Cloud, Nebraska, Percy continued to be an insatiable reader through life. The love of history sent him to scores of volumes in his specialized field and also widened his interest of biography, literature, and travel books. His private library included many sets of history, individual biographies, and Bible commentaries. "I get a great deal of pleasure out of reading good biographies, scientific books of one sort or another," he once said; "and I am passionately fond of studying the Bible and the lives of really great men who have written upon it. This is a kind of avocation with me."

Like most lovers of books, Dr. Percy had his own "system" of organizing them on the shelves of his study. Once his wife set to work arranging the volumes in a logical order, but the results brought consternation to the man. Recounting the incident in mock rage, he said, "Lillian undertook a scientific arrangement of all my books long ago when I didn't know about it. I have been very furious with her, and sick, ever since; because, while they were everything else but scientifically arranged before, yet I knew where every one of them was. The disorder was my great strength in the matter, but the scientific part of it beats me."

The doctor relieved the monotony of train travel by hours of reading, and he consumed scores of books on his journeys to and from the east coast. Among the many volumes he mentions are biographies and autobiographies of Sir William Osler, David Livingstone, Robert Moffat, Winston Churchill, Roger Williams, the Mayo brothers, John Tyndale, Dr. Hans Zinsser, Florence Nightingale, and Warren Harding. When Drs. Percy and Lillian were on auto trips, he drove while she read aloud from magazines, such as *The Atlantic* or the then popular *Literary Digest*. He could enjoy a light article from the English comic magazine *Punch* or ponder a medical research report.

This versatility of interests is revealed in the wide range of references and quotations in his writing and speaking. He would recite lines from a Gilbert and Sullivan light opera or quote Latin from Pliny or Juvenal. He was ready to repeat Shakespeare or use a statement from Martin Luther. In an address given in 1940, the doctor quoted from Shakespeare's *Macbeth,* Tennyson's "The Ancient Sage," and Arthur Clough's "Say Not, the Struggle Nought Availeth." Again, he might include lines from the American poet Edward Sill or repeat stanzas from the Victorian writer Edward Bulwer Lytton.

A bit of verse which he quoted with a twinkle in his eye was remembered by his students:

Some were born for great things,
And some were born for small,
And of some it's not recorded
Why they were born at all.

A WRITER WHO LOVED WORDS

Magan became interested in writing when he made the world tour with Elder Haskell as his companion-secretary. Since the young man's interests in the life, adventure, and customs of the people could not be woven into the conservative material he helped prepare for the *Review and Herald,* he took copious notes of his travels and wrote them into the lengthy series of around-the-world adventure articles for *The Youth's Instructor,* of which we have already taken note. Here are the first inklings of the imagination, humor, human interest, and unique figures of speech that colored his writing and speaking.

In 1896-97, while a member of the Battle Creek College faculty, Percy wrote a series of articles for the *Review and Herald* on the French Revolution and the lessons it offered the Christian church as it faced the social and political upheavals of the approaching twentieth century. Desiring to bring a sincere, convincing message to his readers, Professor Magan said, "Again and again I ask myself: Is there that power and spirit in what you write that will save a soul from death?"

In later years, Dr. Magan spent many hours delving into the lives of Old Testament characters, for he loved to give inspirational talks on these "storm-tossed and wearied souls," or write their biographies, which "revealed the Father's love." He prepared a series of eight sketches for the *Signs of the Times,* entitled "Lowly Folk of the Great Book." His mellow style of writing is well illustrated in these vignettes.

There is a graciousness in his use of words and a nineteenth-century quality in his figures of speech.

"WORDS, WORDS, WORDS"

Fascinated with words, Dr. Magan decried their misuse or abuse. He once declared, "I have a very deep admiration for English, which to my mind is the most beautiful and expressive language in the world." He deplored the fact that the language in some parts of America was degenerating until it was "a disgrace to any civilized community." Many times in his speeches and sermons he would probe into the etymology of words as a method of enriching and dramatizing their meaning. In emphasizing the attribute of humility, he declared: "This word 'humility' comes from the Latin word *humus,* a term which is oftentimes applied to a soil that is easily broken up." Or he might analyze a word in this manner: " 'Welcome' in the olden days may have been used by the judges by way of greeting the runners who were victorious in the races. They had run well. They had *well come.*"

In his address given at the dedication of the Los Angeles County Hospital, the doctor emphasized the word "hospital." He noted that it is "a name which cometh from the same root word as *hospitality.* It is akin to the word 'hostel,' an old form of our word hotel." Many times his training in Latin at the English boys' schools was used to an advantage, for in the same speech Dr. Percy referred to the word "profession," which, he said, "was endowed with more or less of a spiritual significance in the Middle Ages, It is derived from the Latin *pro,* meaning 'before,' and *fateor,* 'to confess.' The word signifies the act of professing or declaring one's faith."

As a writer of letters Dr. Percy was a master of diplomacy and a keen student of human nature. When corresponding with a veteran churchman, the doctor could use the expressions and clichés common in denominational circles. Thus he would write with understanding, kindness, and restraint. However, when he wrote to a close friend, such as Ed Sutherland, on the same issue, the Irishman "pulled out all of the stops." Sharp witticism, intense reactions, and inner rebellion sometimes poured forth in these intimate epistles. Again, when he wrote to the officials of the American Medical Association, he could, as dean or president, set forth the case for the medical school in suave, heart-warming terms that overcame prejudice and won a host of friends for the institution.

HIS MEDICAL ADDRESSES CENTERED IN THE BIBLE

Sermons and other formal speeches held no terrors for the Irishman. Indeed, he enjoyed speaking to audiences, and in his diary, after many a sermon, he wrote, "I had a good time!" When he spoke on a subject of his choice he simply allowed "the excess from his heart to overflow at the mouth."

Wit and humor flashed frequently when Dr. Percy told his inimitable stories. As one alumnus described it, "I remember how he stood before the class and seemed to turn up his nose and tell us a story." Sometimes the administrator introduced his subject by saying: "I don't belong to the tribe of Levi. I am not a preacher. I don't belong to the tribe of Teachi. I am not a teacher. But I am simply a humble member of the tribe of Mediki."

His two most significant addresses in the realm of medicine were given on November 30, 1931, at the annual meeting of the Association of American Colleges, held in New Orleans, and on April 15, 1934, at the dedication of the Acute Unit of Los Angeles County Hospital. While these talks were prepared for secular occasions, the doctor enriched them with quotations and allusions from the Bible.

In the paper read at the New Orleans meeting, Dr. Percy used a New Testament text to epitomize his theme. He said, "In our own hearts' language . . . we are asking ourselves . . . that question which men of an elder day brought forth at the time when John the Baptist was born: '*What manner of child shall this be?*" He also directly quoted Isaiah 32:2; Luke 22:24; John 3:8; and 2 Timothy 2:20. There were dozens of allusions, such as "the angel of death," "the wiles of the devil," "wrestle . . . against spiritual wickedness in high places," "the straight and narrow path," "the seed which we sow will fall on good ground," and "King David of Israel was a man after God's own heart." He referred to Gamaliel, Cain and Abel, the Great Physician, and Calvary. Truly, it was a sermonic masterpiece addressed to physicians at a medical convention!

In the dedicatory address at Los Angeles, the president of C.M.E. again chose a text from the Bible to be his keynote. On this occasion he quoted Joshua 4:6, 7, with emphasis on the question, "*What mean ye by these stones?*" On this occasion he referred directly to Matthew 10:7, 8; 1 Kings 6:7; and 1 Peter 2:5. He ended the dedicatory address with a prayer in which he quoted Isaiah 53:4.

Truly, in his writing and speaking, Dr. Magan was a man of the

Book of books. It was his inspiration, his richest source of beautiful and sonorous language, and the center of his thinking.

SERMON TOPICS LONG REMEMBERED

Some of the unique and stimulating sermon topics mentioned in his diary or remembered by students and faculty are: "If Thou Hast Run With the Footmen," "The Ephah Small and the Shekel Large," "Dead Flies," "The Garrison of the Philistines in the Hill of God," "Horses and Chariots of Fire," "Elisha, the Great Medical-Missionary Prophet," "The Bad Medical Student" (this sermon centered around 2 Kings 5, and revealed how Gehazi failed to learn from the doctor-prophet), "And Lot Pitched His Tent Toward Sodom," "Blood Brotherhood," "The Poorest Man on Earth," and "Don't Lose Sight of Your Vision."

Unusual texts upon which the doctor based some of his unforgettable sermons included Job 15:11: "Are the consolations of God small with thee? is there any secret thing with thee?" and Exodus 13:19: "Moses took the bones of Joseph with him."

"I think his two favorite texts were: 'The little foxes, that spoil the vines' (Song of Solomon 2:15), and 'dead flies cause the ointment of the apothecary to send forth a stinking savor: so doth a little folly him that is in reputation for wisdom and honor' (Ecclesiastes 10:1)," says another alumnus. A sermon given before a senior class on the topic, "The Prayer of Christ," was especially appropriate, for the doctor paraphrased the Master's petition by placing the graduates in the position of the disciples for whom the Saviour prayed.

Writing of the impressions that the doctor's sermons made upon the students, one alumnus lists several special topics: "The first one of these that I recall was from a text found in 1 Kings 3:7, where young Solomon says, 'And now, O Lord my God, Thou hast made Thy servant king instead of David my father: and I am but a little child: I know not how to go out or come in.' Dr. Magan used to tell us that in our schooling it was so important for us to learn how to go out and come in. Not once, but many times, did he use this text to encourage us to learn proper decorum and deportment."

Taking John 10:41, "John did no miracle: but all things that John spake of this Man were true," Dr. Magan enlarged upon the text with these inspiring thoughts: "So very few of us do any miracles. We are pretty helpless. The doctor feels that his life is without miracles. The housewife toils on, and when the evening comes she thinks, 'I did no miracle today.' The student rises to the sound of a bell and retires the same way. Even a missionary lives a monotonous life, and because of hardship feels that he has done no miracle. Let's look back at the text. I am thankful that here is a man who felt that he did no miracle, but still he accomplished something."

Dr. Thomason marveled at the Irishman's versatility. "You are like the stream in your speaking, you go on forever," he once said to Dr. Percy; "and every time I hear you I am always greatly impressed with your tremendous vision of things and your inimitable manner of expressing things." In a tribute to the administrator at the time of his death, Dr. George T. Harding wrote: "Few men have such a gift as Dr. Magan for making the commonplace seem interesting and worthwhile. Even the drudgery of some routine task assumed importance under the magic of his words. From his unlimited storehouse he was able to draw examples, usually from the Bible, to answer and illustrate any question. He knew the Bible as few men do and applied its lessons in his daily living.

"Who will ever forget his sermon based on Solomon's reply to God's request, 'Ask what I shall give thee' in 1 Kings 3? He began by saying, 'And I am but a little child: I know not how to go out or come in.' Seldom do we remember the text and the place of a sermon, but I recall hearing this sermon on the importance of getting along with people first as a freshman at Washington Missionary College in 1920. Like an artist with a brush and a few colors, Dr. Magan could create a thought picture capable of moving the minds and hearts of all to new and higher aspirations and devotions."

The multifarious activities, the tedious hours at the desk or in board and committee session, did not prevent the dedicated man from reading. It was a "must" with him to take time for meditation and prayer. On his lengthy trips he recorded hours of study and prayer in hotel rooms. After a hectic meeting with medical-association officials he frequently sought a quiet retreat to recharge the spiritual battery of his soul. Once he wrote: "The strength and power of our spiritual life may be estimated in terms of the earnest and prayerful study we give to the great Word of God. . . . In studying the mighty Word I have found no greater spiritual help than in the writings of Ellen G. White. . . . They illuminate the great Page; they assist the mind in understanding what is written in the Bible; they cast a gleam of heavenly sunshine across its pages."

19

As His Students Saw Him

When a biographer writes the life of an educator, he finds that the acid test of the man's achievement is in the estimates given him by his students and fellow faculty members. They witness his moods day after day when the niceties wear thin, and where he, as a teacher or administrator, takes the incessant pummeling of petty problems and vital issues.

In preparing this volume, the author sent a questionnaire to twelve hundred C.M.E. alumni who had known Percy Magan during his years of service at the medical school. Some of these physicians sat with "P.T.," as they nicknamed him, on boards and faculty sessions, some were disciplined under his administration, and some had the privilege of intimate association with the Magan family. The response of the alumni to the letter and the questions was a surprise, indeed! Hundreds of replies came from alumni who had been on the campus during the Magan era. A number of doctors took time from their busy practice to write four- or five-page single-spaced typewritten letters. Several physicians typed the answers themselves, explaining that their feelings were too personal to dictate.

As to the character of this physician, there was no doubt of his sincerity, his humility, and his devotion to God and to the medical college. He was remembered by many for his "great Irish smile," his enthusiasm, humor, mental dependability, and flexibility. He possessed "a great sense of timing" and a "warm understanding of human nature."

Although smaller in stature than average, and slightly round-shouldered, he had, as one letter put it, a "pixielike smile," and "the map of Ireland imprinted on his face." He called the students by their first names, or sometimes, for a change, addressed them as "son" or "daughter." As he was remembered, "he carried a dignity about him that is now seldom seen, yet he was not so dignified that he was unapproachable by students." By no means handsome, yet "his immaculate dress and almost saintly mannerisms set him apart. In fact, some of the students thought he would have doubled well for the apostle Paul."

THE ART OF FRIENDSHIP

An intense interest in youth and their success marked him as a genuine educator. Says one who knew him well, "The doctor made us feel that he understood and was sympathetic with our problems, and he seemed to gain a certain amount of delight in seeing us working and struggling for achievement."

A student who suffered a prolonged illness during his days at Los Angeles had this memory of Dr. Percy: When the youth lay for months in the White Memorial Hospital, the busy dean frequently took time to drop in for a bedside visit. "The experience that stands out greatest," says the alumnus, "is the night he came into my room with two other men, one a senior medical student, and the other the Bible professor at the White Memorial division. I had been given up and was considered to be near death, but Dr. Magan considered this an opportunity. I well remember the earnest prayer, after I had been anointed, and as he and the other two men earnestly sought God the feeling came to me that there was nothing more to worry about, that everything would be all right. It was months before I was perfectly well; but Dr. Magan never lost faith, and he always held out encouragement to me."

When there were problems of discipline, the doctor frequently went to the aid of the student in difficulty. This made him, as one alumnus declares, "the friend of the underdog." Yet he never sacrificed principle for sentimentality, and students knew this and respected him for his stand. On one occasion when the faculty was taking a rigid stand concerning the admission of a student, Dr. Magan, who was more lenient in the case, said, "If Ruth the Moabitess had been on the earth at this time and had wanted admittance among the people of God, she never would have gotten it from those fellows. . . . However, the good Lord took Ruth in; . . . and she not only proved herself a good woman, but she became an ancestress of our Lord Jesus Christ."

One graduate, recounting his adventures in romance, relates his experience. In his junior year he and a student nurse went on a date without permission. The girl received moderate discipline, but the medical student was immune to punishment because it was during summer vacation. In relating the course of events, he says: "I volunteered to accept disciplinary action, it not seeming fair for her to be punished and for me to go unpunished. Well, under P.T.'s guidance the faculty threw the book at me. All social privileges were withdrawn for an indefinite period."

The medical student and the nurse were known to be engaged, but the ban on their meeting was rigid. At this time the girl "was on late duty at the operating room . . . and as she had to pass through three blocks of unsavory area at midnight," her fiancé escorted her nightly from surgery to her front door. When this became known to the faculty, Dr. Magan dismissed the medical student from the school. The personal account continues: "My class protested violently, and the action was rescinded and I was reinstated. But I felt the penalties . . . too severe and resigned from the school, and then returned the next fall to graduate. In the meantime the girl and I were married. And where do you think we were married? and by whom? Why, of course, in the home of and by the man we most loved and respected, Percy T. Magan!"

SPEAKING OF MARRIAGE

Many medical students requested Dr. Magan to read the marriage service for their wedding. When an honorarium was offered to the doctor for his part in the ceremony, he usually had a touch of humor in his reply. Said one student, "Dr. Percy tore open the envelope, observed its contents, looked over to the bride, and declared, 'Keep it. If this man does not treat you right, or gives you any trouble, use this money to call me!' " Or again, after another wedding, Dr. Percy turned the fee over to the bride, and with a twinkle in his eyes, he said, "Here, you take this, your husband thinks that's all you are worth."

Another happily married couple look back on the day the doctor performed the ceremony. It was in days of depression, and the best man proffered the doctor a $5 bill. Taking the money, Dr. Percy placed it in the bridegroom's hand. "Take this bill, change it into a $5 gold piece, and do not spend it until after your first quarrel with your wife." The alumnus, in recounting that day, writes: "After thirty years of marriage I still have that $5 gold piece—not necessarily an indication that we have not occasionally had disagreements, but none were ever serious. Consequently, we still have the gold piece!"

Meager finances of the students sometimes dampened youthful dreams of a full-scale wedding. A C.M.E. graduate recounts how Dr. Magan surprised the bride and groom on their nuptial day: "The one outstanding personal experience I had with Dr. Magan was on our wedding day. My wife and I had both been brought up in homes where a penny meant much, for we saw but few of them. We had both worked our way through school. Both her parents and mine lived at different locations in northern California. She was working in the business office at the White Memorial Hospital, and I was a freshman medical student when we first met. After about eighteen months of courtship we decided to marry. Because of our financial status, the anticipated long road ahead, plus the fact that our homes were so far away, my bride-to-be and I decided upon a simple ceremony with our two best friends as our witnesses. I asked Dr. Magan to tie the knot. At the appointed hour, the four of us met in his study where we rather impatiently waited for him to get down to the business of performing the ceremony, but he leisurely chatted with us in his friendly way. Then after what seeemed like a long time, he said that Dr. Lillian and he thought we should have a little music for our wedding and invited us into another room where they had recorded wedding music playing and about twenty-five people seated. So we had a nice little wedding given us by Dr. Magan and his lovely wife."

A VERSATILE STORY TELLER

Tension-relieving humor can be a blessing to relax the weary mind. A well-told story often relieves the stress of pent-up emotions. Dr. Percy achieved the art of story telling during his college days, for students at Battle Creek remembered the anecdotes and humorous tales of his boyhood.

On the medical-school campus the story most frequently mentioned by his students was the occasion when the doctor would address noisy freshman groups. He would pause and ask what "puberty" meant. After some delay the answer would come that "puberty means the change from childhood to manhood." Quickly the Irishman would reply, "The trouble with some of you is that you have come to the age of puberty but you haven't 'pubed' yet!"

The bald-headed Irishman had a sense of humor concerning his own looks. He said that when he was a student at Battle Creek College he admired the long, white hair and flowing beards of the pioneers. "It was my ambition to look like them when I grew old," he declared with a mischievous squint of his eyes. Then he added, "And now look at me!"

When conditions did not work out perfectly or someone did a task that was substandard, he would tell the story of the English vendor who called out, "Hot mutton pies." A customer who sampled the pastry chided the salesman, "I say, mate, this pie is neither hot nor mutton."

"Ah, well," came the reply, "that's just the name of it."

AN UNDERSTANDING ADMINISTRATOR

As the alumni look back upon the years Dr. Percy served as dean or president, what is their opinion of his contribution to the school? Letters from graduates do not hedge on this topic. Their views are well summarized by one statement: "I believe it was his prestige, his steadfastness of purpose, his unwavering confidence that this school must and would, in the light of what he knew, succeed, that was the stablizing influence that carried our struggling medical college through the most critical period of its existence."

As to the man's ability, another graduate declares: "He was the typical Irishman who 'kissed the Blarney stone,' in his reactions to people, and at the same time he was well versed in intrigue. This combination of the soft hand and the knowledge of what makes people tick, allowed him to get along with the American Medical Association and the General Conference. His great ability as a politician brought about a golden era in the history of the C.M.E."

He was at home with all men, whether in medical circles or church groups. Of his ability to meet issues with influential leaders, one alumnus says: "He could sit down with a council on medical education, including the president of the American Medical Association, and discuss matters of medical education, in general, call each man by his first name, and still retain their utmost respect. For the most part, he could think faster than those who were on either side of the fence. He did not let the stupidity of one group blind or irritate him to the point of clouding his thinking. Neither did he let the pressures of the other side push him to the point that he found himself out on a limb. A politician, yes, but always of the finest sort. To my knowledge, I doubt that there was ever a time in his life when he compromised, in any way, with fundamental moral principles."

Tolerance was an attribute he possessed in guiding young people. He once said, "You know, when the good Lord had all the holy angels with Him in heaven, right under His thumb, one third of them went wrong! Now folks expect us [the faculty] to do better than that right here!"

Describing the sincerity of Dr. Percy's religion that permeated his administrative duties, a C.M.E. graduate writes: "He would come into my little office to talk to me, and he never left without having prayer. His prayer was always for the medical students, that they would keep their faith. Even now I can hear the earnestness of those prayers that he offered in the students' behalf. I well recall, one time, when the school needed a Bible professor, the remark that was made which was so characteristic of Dr. Magan. He said, 'If we could only find a Bible teacher who would put his arms around these students and love them into the truth.' On another occasion, he seemed to be interested in the personal experience of the students, and he wanted to know what could be done to encourage them to keep their faith in a definite and personal way. Then he made this remark to me, 'I hope I always have the right influence on the students. In trying to set the right example I have never even so much as gone to a circus. I have tried to eat right, drink right, live right, so that my influence will be right with the medical students.'"

An alumnus recounts how he was personally assisted by the busy administrator. The medical student and his wife had lost their new-born child. In describing the experience, the graduate says: "I was quite discouraged on this particular morning and was sitting on a bench near the place where Dr. Magan would go into the hallway which led to his office. My wife was still in the hospital, and I was enormously in debt. I had no zest for study, and I felt that I was quite forsaken. At this moment Dr. Magan crossed the center court, spoke to me, and I answered him. I heard the door close as he went into the hallway to his offices. Suddenly it reopened, and I can still see his form standing before me, his solemn and understanding eyes, and that unusually long upper lip. His head turned from side to side as he looked intently at me and then came these words: 'You don't look right. Come on in.' I followed him into his office, and as we entered, I saw a great number of people waiting to see him, among them being Dr. Rufus B. Von Kleinschmidt, the Chancellor of U.S.C. As I went into his office he started to talk to me, but soon the telephone rang. He answered it and we talked again. Soon the telephone rang the second time. He answered it. Upon completion of this call he called the operator to please kill his line for ten minutes. Then right face to face and man to man he talked of the discouragements of his own life and how they had been surmounted through the agencies of prayer and faith. And then he prayed with me. Although not a word of my financial condition was mentioned he without asking pressed